LOVABILITY

How to Build a Business That
People Love and Be Happy Doing It

———

BRIAN DE HAAFF

CO-FOUNDER AND CEO OF AHA!

GREENLEAF
BOOK GROUP PRESS

Published by Greenleaf Book Group Press
Austin, Texas
www.gbgpress.com

Distributed by Greenleaf Book Group

This book is available for bulk purchases at a special discount. For more information, please contact Greenleaf Book Group at PO Box 91869, Austin, TX 78709, (512) 891-6100 or by email at orders@greenleafbookgroup.com.

Design by Aha! Labs Inc., Greenleaf Book Group, and Sheila Parr

Publisher's Cataloging-In-Publication Data
(Prepared by The Donohue Group, Inc.)
de Haaff, Brian.
    Lovability : How to build a business that people love and be happy doing it /
        Brian de Haaff, founder and CEO of AHA!
Austin, Texas : Greenleaf Book Group Press, [2017] | Includes bibliographical references and index.
    LCCN 2016955016 | ISBN 978-1-62634-403-7 (print) | ISBN
        978-1-62634-404-4 (ebook)
LCSH: Consumer satisfaction. | Customer loyalty. | Product design--Psychological aspects. | Technological innovations. | Success in business. | Love.
LCC HF5415.335 .D44 2016 (print) | LCC HF5415.335 (ebook) | DDC 658.8/343--dc23

Part of the Tree Neutral® program, which offsets the number of trees consumed in the production and printing of this book by taking proactive steps, such as planting trees in direct proportion to the number of trees used: www.treeneutral.com

Printed in the United States of America on acid-free paper

17 18 19 20 21 22   10 9 8 7 6 5 4 3 2

For my love, Michelle, and our industrious builders
Zachary, Jason, and Noah

CONTENTS

Part I

GRANDPA-INSPIRED

INTRODUCTION

I ride my bike a few times a week through the campus of Stanford University. It's about a mile from my house, and it sits more or less at the epicenter of Silicon Valley both physically and psychologically. Even as a proud graduate of The University of California at Berkeley, I acknowledge that it is one of the most prestigious universities in the world. It also hosted one of the more important speeches on innovation in recent memory.

On March 31, 2016, Securities and Exchange Commission chair Mary Jo White said this to the students of Stanford Law School:

> Nearly all venture valuations are highly subjective. But, one must wonder whether the publicity and pressure to achieve the unicorn benchmark is analogous to that felt by public companies to meet projections they make to the market with the attendant risk of financial reporting problems. And, yes that remains a problem. We continue to see instances of public companies and their senior executives manipulating their accounting to meet various expectations and projections.[1]

We have reached a point in the world of technology startups where the fervor for building a company with a billion-dollar valuation — the elusive startup unicorn — is overshadowing the creation of real value. It is not the first time we have been here; the world of startups and venture capital has always run in cycles, from optimistic zeal to caution to post-catastrophe introspection and back again. But perhaps it is time that entrepreneurs and investors alike begin waking up to the fact that the "valuation-at-all-costs" model, with its relentless pressure, remote odds of success, and human cost, is not only unsustainable but bad business.

At this point in the current cycle, the radically overvalued startup appears to be headed for the endangered species list. That is a good thing. While billion-dollar behemoths will always exist, and the high-wire act of chasing scale while also chasing the cash to *fund* that scale will occasionally produce a solid company, there are other ways to build a business. There are *better* ways to build a business.

A Tale of Two Companies

If you have kids, you are probably tired of hearing about Minecraft, the 3D sandbox role-playing game created by Swedish programmer Markus "Notch" Persson and released in its full-featured form in 2011. Persson did not create Minecraft because he wanted to create a billion-dollar company; he loved video games and kept his day job while developing it. When the game soared in popularity, he started a company, Mojang, with some of the profits, but kept it small, with just 12 employees.

Even with zero dollars spent on marketing and no user instructions, Minecraft grew exponentially, flying past the 100 million registered user mark in 2014 based largely on word of mouth.[2] Players shared user-generated extras like modifications ("mods") and custom maps with each other, and the game caught on not only with children but their parents and even educators. Still, Persson avoided the valuation game, refusing an investment offer from former Facebook president Sean Parker. Finally, he and his co-founders sold Mojang to Microsoft for $2.5 billion, a fortune built on one man's focus on creating something that people loved.[3]

On the other end of the spectrum is Zynga, one of the fastest startups ever to reach a $1 billion valuation.[4] The social game developer had its first hit in 2009 with FarmVille. Next came Zynga's partnership with Facebook that turned into a growth engine. The company began trading on the NASDAQ in December 2011 and had 253 million active users per month as late as the first quarter of 2013.[5] Then the relationship with Facebook ended and the wheels started coming off.

Flush with IPO cash, Zynga started exhibiting all the symptoms of ego-driven, grow-at-any-cost syndrome. They moved into a $228 million headquarters in San Francisco. They began hastily acquiring companies like NaturalMotion, Newtoy, and Area/Code. They infuriated customers by launching new games without sufficient testing and filling them with scripts that signed players up for unwanted subscriptions and services. When customer outrage went viral, instead of focusing on building better products, Zynga hired a behavioral psychologist to try to trick customers into loving its games.[6]

In a 2009 speech at Startup@Berkeley, CEO Mark Pincus said, "I funded [Zynga] myself but I did every horrible thing in the book to just get revenues right away. I mean, we gave our users poker chips if they downloaded this Zwinky toolbar, which . . . I downloaded it once — I couldn't get rid of it. We did anything possible just to just get revenues so that we could grow and be a real business."[7]

By the spring of 2016, Zynga had laid off about 18 percent of its workforce and its share price had declined from $14.50 in 2012 to about $2.50.

Back to Basics

Zynga's story provides an important caution, and Minecraft's is a positive sign. We are coming back around to a healthy part of the business cycle where the focus is on building solid products and creating customer value. The founders of would-be high-flying startups are being regarded with greater skepticism while businesspeople who operate like our grandparents did — by building on relationships, quality, and value creation — are thriving.

The signs of this change are everywhere:

- According to *The Wall Street Journal,* after a two-year funding binge that inflated startup valuations, venture investors have closed their wallets. Funding for U.S. startups fell in the first quarter of 2016 by 25 percent to $13.9 billion, the biggest quarterly decline since the dot-com bubble burst in 2001.[8]

- Mutual fund giant Fidelity whispered that unicorns might be mythical when it marked down the value of its holdings in companies like Dropbox, Zenefits, CloudFlare, and DocuSign in early 2016. A *Bloomberg* article about the write-downs said, "Investors still have high hopes for corporate software companies to go public this year. But in some cases, the expectations may have lost touch with reality at many startups raising money in 2014 and 2015."[9]

- In his March 2016 *Term Sheet* newsletter, Dan Primack commented that IPO activity in the technology sector was nonexistent. "The window might not be closed, but it sure does seem abandoned," he wrote.[10] According to CNN Money, there were no U.S. tech IPOs in the first quarter of 2016, the first time that has happened since 2009.[11]

- The compensation gravy train has derailed. Former highfliers like Dropbox have cut perks and advised employees to start saving their money. Startups are having trouble finding new hires as workers; spooked by concerns about revenues, would-be applicants choose to stay with sure things rather than chase stock option gold.

- The idea of putting customers first and acting with integrity is gaining traction. Outdoor-gear retailer REI received adulation for adhering to its values when it announced that it would not only close its stores on Black Friday in 2015 but pay its employees to get outside. Contrast that with blood-test startup Theranos. CEO Elizabeth Holmes was lauded as "America's youngest self-made billionaire,"[12] and the firm was quickly valued at $9 billion. Then, testing showed that the company's flagship Edison device, which purported to deliver test results from a single drop of blood, did not work.[13] The federal government swiftly began investigating Holmes, with regulators not only revoking the company's license to operate but suggesting a ban preventing Holmes from owning or operating a lab for two years. Walgreens Boot Alliance Inc. sued Theranos for $140 million, equivalent to the amount the drugstore giant had invested in the startup.[14] In the fall of 2016, Theranos announced it would be shutting down its blood-testing facilities and shed at least 40 percent of its workforce.[15]

- The 2016 Technology Vision report from Accenture, which identified the key developing trends in the digital world, was titled, "People First." It offered a simple but revolutionary message: Business is not about software or hardware, but the people who create value.[16]

- Profit is the new black. Asked for the advice he'd give to startup founders, Under Armour CEO Kevin Plank told attendees at a 2016 panel talk, "Losing money is cultural. It's a habit. If you get used to losing money, it's really hard to stop . . . if I have advice for an entrepreneur today, go out and find out if your product can sell."[17]

We have fallen out of love with the cycle of excessive hype with no meaningful results from emerging companies. As one investor in the now-defunct Shuddle, which was positioned as "Uber for kids," said, "Last year investors were turned on by growth; this year people want to understand how and when you will make money!"[18] Dreams of personal wealth have given way to the harsh reality that businesses built on hype rarely yield returns. The fundamentals — people, service, relationships, transparency, trust — are becoming sexy again. Why? Because they produce results.

A Different Kind of Company

A human-centered approach is consistent with the time-tested values of our grandparents and the way they did business. Those values inspired Dr. Chris Waters and me to found our company, Aha!

Chris is a technical genius with a PhD and 16 patents. We met in 2005, when I worked at Network Chemistry, a wireless security company that he founded. I had a lot of experience bringing products to market and defining new categories of technology, so I came on board as Vice President of Products and Marketing.

As time went on, it became clear to both of us that the company needed to concern itself less with growth and more with profitability. That meant getting back to its roots and doing one thing exceptionally well. The board of diretors promoted me to the CEO position in 2007 at age 35, and later that year Aruba Networks acquired Network Chemistry. Chris and I had turned our belief in the value of a profitable, back-to-basics approach to business into a friendship. After helping with the transition post-acquisition, we decided to start a new company.

Later that year, we launched Paglo, one of the first IT management companies built on a software-as-a-service (SaaS) platform. We grew Paglo by relying on many of the old-school principles we admired, but since we used outside financing to grow the company we weren't yet able to incorporate them all. Then in 2010, Citrix acquired Paglo. We ran strategy and product development for a major Citrix product line until March 2013. By then, Chris and I had both clocked time in two worlds — developing products for a substantial technology company with a very large cloud-based business and building traditional Silicon Valley startups — and decided that neither one was what we really wanted.

We disliked the time in a big company that was spent managing perceptions. We disliked the lack of transparency and responsiveness and loss of customer understanding. We also disliked the growth-by-hype mentality that infected so many startups, which is also a form of perception management by and for investors. We wanted to do something different, something true. We wanted to be free to focus on creating real customer value and a company without friction. We wanted to build a software company that would help customers do the same thing in their own companies and enjoy it. But we knew that people were struggling to set clear business strategy and connect it to the work of building award-winning products. There was an opportunity to take everything we had learned doing the same and build a product that would help people set goals and initiatives and connect it to the execution. We would build software that would help create a world of awesome products and happy product builders.

We also wanted to create a place where people would love to work. We had too many friends at technology companies who were burning out and checking out. We were tired of investors who put greed before dignity and human well-being. We were well acquainted with the startup model that had been celebrated in Silicon Valley since the mid-1990s, and we knew there had to be a better way to fund our vision than chasing venture capital and trying to manufacture scale with no substance.

Our goals did not seem unreasonable. All we wanted was to . . .

- Create software that would help others build better products.
- Share information freely and remove friction.
- Eliminate traditional approaches to selling.
- Take care of our customers and use technology to interact with them, not avoid them.
- Set smart employees free to be their best and honor their ambition and action.
- Take a long-term outlook and not obsess about get-rich-quick exit strategies.
- Redefine what a technology company could be.

We knew our ideas were ambitious. Making them a reality would be an adventure, but it would be *our* adventure. On April Fool's Day 2013, we set out to make them happen.

Grandpa-Inspired

We built our product strategy and roadmapping software and started a closed, invitation-only Beta. I spoke with and demonstrated Aha! to more than 500 product development teams. People took to both our product and our personal, responsive approach. Chris and I also drew a line in the sand and agreed that we would not hire anyone until we had 100 paying enterprise customers. It was important that we prove that we could create real customer value before complicating the business.

We signed up 125 paying enterprise customers in four months.

Our early success was validation not only that we had built a meaningful product, but that our "grandpa-inspired" way of doing things was working. It gave us the confidence to start growing our team. We did so through profits. We felt justified in believing that more customer value would lead to higher profits. That plus our long-term philosophy meant there was no need to seek outside capital to fund the company. We also stuck to another agreement: We would hire the best people regardless of where they lived. Everyone would work remotely and we would use Aha! to build Aha! We would depend on web video conferences to collaborate internally and support customers. We still operate that way today.

Today we are humbled not only by our continued growth, but by the feedback that we get from customers. In all my years at other companies, I never saw customers express the kind of gratitude and intense appreciation that we hear every day at Aha! We receive a continual stream of sincere, insightful emails from our customers. This is my favorite one. I smile every time I read it, because I know this pain, and we helped eliminate it:

> "I have inherited a product of roughly the same size and complexity of Aha! that was planned using a Ouija board, a small flock of chickens wandering around and selecting agile user stories by defecating upon Post-It notes, and random hacking efforts. The documentation is stored in several hundred PowerPoint presentations, Excel documents, and OneNote pages, none of which can be located except by the person who prepared them for one meeting or another. There is also

documentation, an anti-trail of emails, instant messages, hallway conversations, and whiteboard exercises. I have a paper in peer review at this moment demonstrating that much of the dark matter in the Universe is actually formed by this invisible requirement repository."

He went on to explain that he was rapidly building out his product plans in Aha! and was going to share them with his boss, who was the director of project management. Guess what? No more wandering chickens — his fantasy about working for a company that valued meaningful product planning became a reality.

Not all customer notes are as funny as that one, but most are just as heartfelt. Our old-fashioned way of doing business — which we named The Responsive Method — is making a difference for real people, and that has been our goal from the beginning.

That impact is borne out by the data (all numbers current when this book went to press):

- We have more than 100,000 users on the Aha! platform.
- We have enjoyed more than 10,000 percent revenue growth rate since 2013.
- Since 2013, customers have told us they "love" us more than 2,500 times via phone, email, social networks, and instant messaging.

Lovability

The last item really surprised us. Chris and I had already built several successful products and companies before Aha!, and we know that it is tough to create a compelling strategy and build a product that matters. We figured that if we worked hard there was a good chance we would do well. But our customers' emotional response to our software and our approach caught us completely off guard.

Nobody loves business software or the companies that build it. They tolerate it. People love consumer goods and services, but not software. Software is a necessary evil. But practically since the day we rolled out Aha!, customers have been sending us "love notes" telling us how delighted they are with our product and how we treat them.

We were shocked and flattered . . . and then we decided to start tracking the instances when a customer told us they loved us. A pattern emerged. For example, in 2015 nearly 800 people told us they loved us, an increase of nearly 450 percent over 2014. That number correlated almost perfectly to our 2014 – 2015 growth rate.

Obviously we were on to something. That something, which we call *lovability*, is the reason I wrote this book. Love is the surprising emotion that companies can no longer afford to ignore.

Lovability is the metric that nobody in business talks about but that's obvious in hindsight. Lovability — the capacity to earn genuine, heartfelt love and loyalty from customers — is the secret ingredient that propels a select few organizations ahead and leads not only to consistent growth and profitability but sustainable happiness for everyone involved.

Why is this only obvious in hindsight? Because we do not think about "loving" a product as being a legitimate metric of its success. Too many of us are busy obsessing over vanity numbers, from unique visitors, to trials, to product engagement. But we should put love at center stage, because what is more important to a business's long-term success than customers loving and being loyal to it?

In this book, I have reverse-engineered thousands of customer love letters to reveal what we did to inspire that feeling. I have turned that information into an action plan that readers can use to build lovable products that receive similar levels of passion and devotion. However, lovable products come from lovable companies. The two are inseparable. So while my focus is on products, I will also talk about what makes companies lovable — by not only their customers but their employees — as well.

There has never been a better time for business leaders to explore the potential of creating lovable products, because the relationship between companies and their customers is changing rapidly. The behavior of businesses that I have already talked about — as well as well-publicized customer service fiascos (like Costco's transition to only accept Visa credit cards, which led to more than 1.5 million customer service calls and scathing online complaints[19]) — shows that customers feel let down again and again by the companies they depend on, whether by overreaching marketing claims, pushy sales tactics, terrible customer support, or poor quality.

Combine that with the ever-growing range of customer choices in many product and service categories and their power via online reviews and we may be at a "change or die" inflection point in many industries. Lovable products, services, and companies are disrupting entire industries. They are changing the world.

Back to People

Here is another secret that should not be secret at all: Companies are not brands, buildings, or technology. They are people. A corporation does not do anything; its people and customers do. We need to get back to the human aspect of business. It all starts with people and human interactions.

At Aha!, we help people build better products. As we do, we are seeing a change in how some people are doing that, especially in the world of technology. The current political and business climate has highlighted a conflict between those who manage perceptions and those who pursue achievement — a conflict between spin and reality, hype and performance, empty style and meaningful substance. By focusing on manipulating perceptions instead of achieving meaningful goals, many entrepreneurs are crushing their companies and wasting their potential.

Meaningful achievement, substance, and value may not seem glamorous, but when you have them, they tell their own story. There is no need to manipulate the customer or spin the data. That is why the businesses that have them are not only sustainable but thriving in this new environment.

My goal with this book is to give you a clear path to building products and a business that customers love. Twenty years' experience in Silicon Valley building disruptive software companies has shaped me. Everything I have learned went into Aha!, which has been unbelievably satisfying and rewarding. I want to share the methodology that has made our software company one of the fastest growing in the field and increased happiness for the people who build products and the people who use them. In particular, I want to help product managers and owners change the business landscape one product at a time.

I want to help people find the courage to build products the way they think is right, rather than getting sucked in by the "home-run mentality" of hype, personal fortunes, and chasing scale and valuation at any cost. There are no niches when it comes to building products that people depend on, no matter how large or small your market. If you are solving a real problem, your product and you are changing the world and your customers.

I also want to share the story of The Responsive Method (TRM), the secret of our growth and the engine behind our customer love. TRM is the key to creating lovability. It is a conscious approach that questions everything you have likely learned about how a product gets built and how people connect with it. It is a human approach, driven by the needs of people, not titles, business processes, or "how it's always been done." It is a relationship-based approach guided by the same ideals that guide healthy relationships in other parts of our lives — honesty, empathy, communication, and authenticity.

I hope these insights will advance the career prospects of everyone who reads this book by teaching them about tools and approaches that few know but that work extremely well. I would like to see more businesses become places where employees can find greater purpose and grow. I would like to see fewer subpar products on the market. I would like to see more profitable, growing companies staffed by fulfilled, sustainably happy people building great products and feeling that they are part of something exceptional.

> "We need to get back to the human aspect of business. It all starts with people and human interactions."

I would even like to spark interest in a "lovability economy" and show why it is not only practical but desirable to build businesses around integrity, human happiness, long-term sustainable prosperity, and mutually beneficial exchanges of value. In a rapidly changing world, it is time for a new recipe for success. Lovability may be that recipe.

Who This Book Is for

This book is for you if you care about building a product and business that customers really care deeply about and that you will be happy working on. We have been able to do that by pioneering the use of TRM, and it is having a positive impact. It has been validated by thousands of Aha! customers and hundreds of thousands of people who use our software and follow the company.

We are continually asked to share our approach with startups and established companies alike. And so, this book is for anyone creating a product or service and serving customers. If you work with and sell to human beings, this material applies to you. TRM works for anyone who wants to have a positive impact on their customers and life.

This book was written for . . .

- Startup founders and company builders. We will spend a lot of time here addressing emerging technology companies because we know you well and have built multiple successful startups ourselves.
- Leaders at established companies. We know that you are eager to transform how you innovate and serve customers. CEOs, you are ultimately responsible for the business. You set its vision and allocate budget and resources. VPs of product and digital strategists, you are in charge of strategy and positioning your products in the market. Engineering directors, you and your teams are the ones who make the product roadmap a reality. You all face different challenges and have different skills to contribute, but you are all transforming your company and the markets you serve in compelling ways. We will show you a way to innovate and

build product that has been extraordinarily successful. It is not the only way, and even if it is not a perfect fit for your industry, you should be able to glean something useful from what we have learned.

In both new and old companies, product managers are the people most responsible for making products lovable. Product managers, we have a soft spot in our hearts for you. We get you. You control your company's future because you control its ideas. We know the challenges you face and the talented people in engineering, sales, and marketing that you are expected to lead (without them actually reporting to you). We also know that you have the greatest job in the world, and one of the toughest. This book is for you.

WE LOVE PRODUCT MANAGERS

Why pay special attention to product managers? Because you are the people who nurture products on a day-to-day basis and lead cross-functional teams that can create or destroy customer delight. You collect all your company's ideas, set strategy, create prioritized roadmaps, and keep everyone in sync. We have lived your life. We are one of you.

Product managers are the connection between customers and the engineers who build the product. You are a bridge between what customers say and what the organization actually builds. You sit at the epicenter of everyone in your organization who builds, markets, sells, and supports your product. You explain what engineering is building to the people in sales and support. You interact with legal. You interact with finance. You are the ambassador for your products inside and outside the company. You are everything.

This book is about helping you do the noble work of building products with conviction. It is about discovering (or re-discovering) your *mojo* — that sense of potency, confidence, and swagger that you have when you say to yourself, "I've got this."

If you are reading this book, you want to be the best. You want to build more than a product; you aspire to build a masterpiece, something you can still be proud of when you are old. You feel there must be a better, more human-centric way to build products than what makes the headlines, but something is holding you back. Maybe you are just starting to build a new product but have never known a different way to do it. Perhaps you are stuck in an organization with weak strategy, poor communications, and people who have lost their way.

Whatever is holding you back, we get it. We're offering you a hand to help break through — or break free. After all, life is short. Why spend it doing anything less than meaningful work with people you care about? Let us help you find even greater inspiration and a few new approaches to be your best. Let's start building.

Part II

WHY BUILD LOVABLE PRODUCTS?

♡ *Chapter One*

WHAT IS A PRODUCT?

In the history of e-commerce companies, Ebates is practically prehistoric, having been around since 1998. In a world where early dot-com stalwarts from Boo.com to Digital Entertainment Network have become cautionary tales, Ebates is doing something right. That something has nothing to do with technology or the company's brand and everything to do with trust.

The company's business model is built around the relationships it maintains with about 2,600 retailers ranging from Rite Aid to Ralph Lauren. When customers enter the Ebates online mall, the site directs them to a store based on their needs. They make their purchases, merchants pay a percentage of the order to Ebates, and Ebates returns some of that to the customer. Retailers get well-qualified customer traffic, the customer is rewarded for shopping through Ebates, and Ebates gets a piece of that commerce. But it would not work without trust.

To find out how building customer trust factored into their path of growth, I spoke with Serge Doubinski, Senior Director of Product at Ebates. He said that customers are frequently surprised by the seemingly "too good to be true" value of Ebates. And he told me that's why customer support is baked into everything from the CEO's office down to individual phone support personnel. Customer support builds value and trust for existing members. Ebates's ability to support customers as they shop online is essential, especially because of the many merchants and systems involved in getting them their savings and money back.

"Customer support is part of development for us, a shared metric across multiple teams," he said. "It's not an afterthought. Our customer support team might focus on the number of support tickets we're receiving and how to resolve them, but when we are developing a solution, everyone — from our product managers to our directors — is talking and thinking about customer support. How many tickets can this feature help resolve? How can our product development efforts make our customers' experience better?"

The payoff? In 2014 Japanese e-commerce giant Rakuten acquired Ebates for $1 billion.[1]

Complete Product Experience

Businesses like Ebates have a holistic view of what constitutes their product, but they are the exceptions to the rule. When most companies think of a product, they think only of the thing that they directly sell. Customers focus on what is marketed and what they will use. With software, that means the features they interact with on their computer, tablet, or smartphone screen. For a website like Ebates, the product is the website where users go to shop. For a physical product like a smartphone, it is the thing they hold in their hand. But that is a narrow definition that leads businesses to see only part of the truth.

Let's look at Ebates again. At first glance, the product might seem to be the website. But that is not really what the customer values, even if they do not realize it consciously. They value the rebates they receive and the opportunity to gain financially from shopping with companies they already respect. But what they value most of all is what makes the entire exchange possible: trust. Customers trust that Ebates will deliver on its promises while keeping their information secure. That, more than anything else, is why the company sold for so much money.

In any business, but especially in technology, your product is not just the software or hardware that you ship or the basic service that you provide. It is not just the bits or even the tangible item that the clerk hands over the counter or that arrives at the customer's home. The product is the complete experience and the relationship you and the customer share. That creates loyalty, trust, and love. That is your product. That is the Complete Product Experience (CPE).

I am not the first person to talk about the CPE, and Aha! is not the first company to make it the cornerstone of its brand. In its television ad campaign, Discover Card — taking a subtle dig at its larger rivals — promises that when you call them you will talk to a real person. What's more, the campaign indicates that customer support representative will listen, understand you, and not try to sell you anything. In the commercial, the customer and the customer support rep are played by the same actor. The message is clear: *We care about you* just like you care about you.

Discover is selling the entire experience of carrying one of their credit cards, not just the plastic. Too often, such businesses are treated as outliers when they should be seen as thought leaders. The concept of the CPE gets marginalized and even ignored because it challenges product builders to work harder and leaders to think broader.

Harvard economist Theodore Levitt was the first authority to write about what he called the *total product*.[2] A total product has four dimensions that marketers, executives, and support people need to understand if they want customers to appreciate the value of what they are selling:

1. **Generic**
   What your product is — software, a suitcase, etc.

2. **Expected**
   The essential features and benefits the product must provide, e.g., a refrigerator has to cool food.

3. **Value-Added**
   Features and benefits that exceed customer expectations.

4. Potential

Future enhancements to value based on what customers want.

Levitt's thinking was daring but limited because it focused on features and benefits but not the overall customer experience. Then in 1999, Geoffrey A. Moore took Levitt's ideas to the next logical level with his book, *Crossing the Chasm*. According to Moore, the way to create a "whole" product is to think through both your customer's problems and solutions. It's not enough to address the core product — you have to think about everything needed to get your customer from consideration to an imperative to buy. This can be everything from the installation of the product to training to procedural standards to integrations, whether they are provided by your company or achieved using partners.[3]

> "The product is the complete experience and the relationship you and the customer share."

Moore moved beyond features and benefits — bigger iPhones with higher camera resolution — to something else: Being the solution to customers' problems. Doing that requires more than visionary engineers and brilliant designers. It means getting to know your customers, learning what they care about, and learning to care about them. That's why Moore is the grandfather of the CPE.

Redefining Product

In the era when digital, app-based, cloud-based, and Internet-based products dominate the marketplace, lots of companies are giving into the temptation to turn the customer experience over to technology. On the surface this makes sense, because it limits "costly" person-to-person interactions. That is a grave mistake. Customers want human interaction, and increasingly, they are making it a deal breaker.

A 2016 Accenture Strategy report, "Digital Disconnect in Customer Engagement," found that 83 percent of U.S. consumers prefer dealing with human beings over digital tools to solve customer service issues. Fifty-two percent have left a service provider in the past year due to poor customer service, at an estimated cost of $1.6 trillion. Not enough attention is being paid to managing all customer touch points — the CPE.[4]

It is time that we redefined what we mean when we talk about product. From the point of view of the executive, marketer, or product manager, there are two versions of the word.

- **Product**: What the customer *thinks* they are paying for.

- **CPE**: The totality of what the customer really values and is expecting from a product over the long term.

Today's customer expects every touch point with the technology and the company that sells it to be a meaningful one that creates value. The software-as-a-service (SaaS) world offers a perfect example. Software delivered via the cloud as SaaS is not purchased but rented. Customers pay for it a month or a year at a time. If you understand that, you are more likely to think about delivering it like an ongoing service instead of a one-time sale. Remember, the last S in SaaS stands for *service*.

In that world, you do not just make a sale and walk away any more than you would if you rented a house to someone. You form a relationship with the user of your service. If you want to create lasting value for that customer — and lasting value for your business — you must maintain a mutually beneficial relationship. That takes personal contact, responsiveness, and attention to every stage of the CPE.

The Seven Components

In the world of software and technology, the CPE has seven main components, presented here in a rough order that shows the typical product adoption process. However, the reality is that customers tend to adopt products unpredictably, according to their own tastes and priorities. An organization must be flexible enough to handle multiple adoption paths while staying focused on delivering a high-quality, lovable CPE.

The seven components of the CPE are . . .

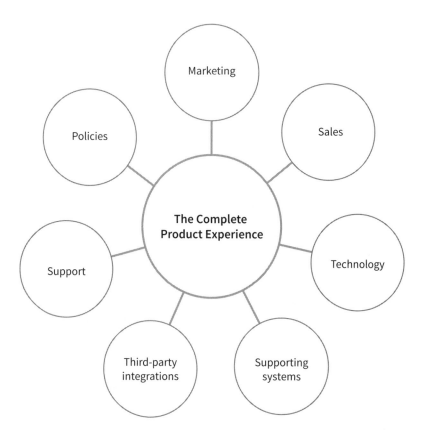

1. **Marketing** is how potential customers learn about your product and determine if it might be a fit to help them solve their problem. This is taking on new forms as people grow increasingly connected: social platforms, online reviews, and company-published content.
2. **Sales** is the process of prospects learning more about the product from a company representative and possibly using it in a trial. They educate

themselves about the product and get the information they need to determine if the solution is right for them.

3. **Technology** refers to the core set of features that customers pay for. In our case, that is the online software that they log into our servers to use. For others it could be the actual phone, credit card, or even an insurance policy that is purchased. However, technology should represent not the *end* of a transaction but the *beginning* of a transparent, interactive relationship.

4. **Supporting systems** make it possible to deliver the product. These are internal systems that the customer rarely sees but which can have a huge impact on their overall happiness: billing, provisioning, analytics, and more. For example, if you call customer support and the representative always seems to have a comprehensive history of your purchases and support issues at their fingertips, you can thank supporting systems.

5. **Third-party integrations** enable new products to fit into how the customer already lives and works. All products exist in an ecosystem, so they have to play nice with the other products the customer is already using and the way that customer already works.

6. **Support** is everything from answering customer questions to training, and even helping customers integrate your product with their existing systems. Support describes all activity that helps the customer achieve something meaningful with a product.

7. **Policies** are the rules that companies set to govern how they do business. At their best they provide a framework for employees to be their best. At their worst, they create unresolvable frustration that drives customers to ask "to speak with the manager."

SUCCESS, NOT SALES

At Aha!, we do not believe that traditional sales processes and people are best suited to serve today's well-informed customers because they are not incented to do so. That is why we have replaced Sales with Customer Success. I will talk more about what that means in chapter 7.

You can divide these components roughly into *technology, people, process,* and *information.* If your goal is to build a sizable, growing customer base and a company culture that powers consistent, sustainable growth, you cannot separate the four. Your customer experience *is* your product, and that experience depends on how effectively you align the technology, people, processes, and information that encompass it.

Why the CPE Matters

In corporate circles you rarely hear anyone talking about all of the aspects of the CPE or how to measure what customers think of them. It is messy, human, and imprecise. Most people prefer high-level conversations and traditional metrics, which provide what appears to be a predictable snapshot of reality. That thinking belongs to the past, when customers had fewer choices and businesses had their hands on the product delivery chain from beginning to end.

Today, technology is increasingly commoditized. Customers have endless choices, more products are self-service, and adoption of them is more transactional. In almost any vertical of today's universe of technology, there are many gifted teams putting bits together in terrific ways that deliver value.

> "If you want to create lasting value for that customer —
> and lasting value for your business — you must maintain
> a mutually beneficial relationship."

In this environment, your features will not set your company apart. Meaningful person-to-person interactions — the CPE — will differentiate you from your competitors. A customer might choose you for your software's eye-popping features list. However, that customer will stay with you for the long haul instead of switching to one of your competitors. They may even enthusiastically send you dozens of new customers. Why? Because you give them an experience that makes them happy while offering reassurance that you will continue to deliver even more happiness in the future. If you are a market leader (or aspire to be one), delivering a lovable CPE is *mandatory*.

Customer Journey Mapping

That is a monumental task, to be sure. Fortunately, there are powerful tools designed to help you understand your CPE, even if you are completely new to the concept. You may already be familiar with the customer journey map, a visual diagram that tracks all the ways your customers engage with your company over time, from their experience with your website to contact with customer support. A customer journey map is a great way to blend analytical data (web traffic, churn rates) and anecdotal data (customer stories, accounts from support teams) into a complete picture that answers a big question: How are our customers experiencing our company and where are we failing to deliver a lovable experience?

There is no one right way to create a customer journey map, but there's a plethora of tools available to you to help you create and manage yours. It is worth the time. The only way to get the CPE right is to have a deep understanding of the customer and to map their journey across every single touch point within your company.

I suggest that you think about your customer's journey as a unified experience that has three key phases: *motivation*, *education*, and *adoption*. Motivation refers to the reasons your prospective customer has for seeking you out and the potential needs your product can satisfy. It also asks the question, "What experiences or emotions motivate the customer to move to the next stage of the journey?" Answering that question helps you provide what the customer needs to progress to the next phase, education.

At this point, the customer chooses from among a wealth of possible options for learning about your products and your company, from reading online reviews and engaging on social media to reviewing your company's documentation and maybe even signing up for a free trial. In the education stage, every business strives to accomplish two goals: *control the message* and *prevent confusion*. Your website and support resources should be easy to use, comprehensive, and invite interaction because you want them to be your customer's first choice. Unlike with Yelp or Twitter, when customers are interacting directly with you it is easy to share information you know is accurate, up-to-date, and relevant. That prevents the confusion that keeps people from buying.

Mapping the final phase, adoption, reveals the experiences that convince customers to buy and those that frustrate them into giving up. What makes people take the plunge? How long does it take and why? How can you accelerate the adoption process without compromising the customer experience?

Suzanne Vaughan, who ran Customer Success at Aha! and is now an executive coach, shares a story about working to understand the motivational journey toward Aha! by a big global software company — $560 million in revenues with 30,000 customers in 60 countries — that intended to build its own in-house product roadmapping solution. Suzanne talks about the time invested to learn about the customer's journey and earn their trust:

> The new CEO, who had started in January of 2014, had set "clear, concise roadmaps" as his first-year goal. They had a 2015 budget and were planning to build their own solution. A group of three women within the company saw that this would not only mean building a product outside their core competency but all the ongoing cost and maintenance that goes along with that. They preempted that plan when one of the women, a portfolio/practice manager working at a startup inside the company, tried Aha! She knew we would not only help her team

but could be the solution they needed to accomplish the new CEO's agenda.

That was only the beginning of the journey, however. We invested hours of consultation and training to help them effectively structure their products, processes, and workflows. We trained more than 100 people on how to use Aha! and were invited as experts to consult during their internal trainings using their company's own product data. Our consultation went beyond using Aha! and into best practices on product structure, communication to stakeholders, and navigating traditional, agile, and hybrid methodologies.

They signed up for Aha! exactly two months after the portfolio/practice manager first signed up for a trial and chose to keep it under the radar so that corporate IT was not involved. This became common among large, complex companies to temporarily avoid the delay caused by security assessments or legal and procurement processes.

This company also became our blueprint for how to serve larger, complex organizations. In part, that's also how our Enterprise+ plan (which includes our highest level of support and training) was born. And because we wanted to ensure that new team members could readily access live training, this also was the beginning of the Customer Success team scheduling group demos as "refreshers" or "maintenance training" for groups of our customers.

Understanding the customer's journey and need at a deep level led not only to a purchase of our software but actually transformed both the customer's internal culture and our own. Thinking broadly about the CPE led both companies to develop a worldview well beyond just thinking about technology. That's what leads to love, loyalty, and profitability.

Customer Journey Map

This is an example of a customer journey map that you can recreate to determine how lovable your Complete Product Experience (CPE) is.

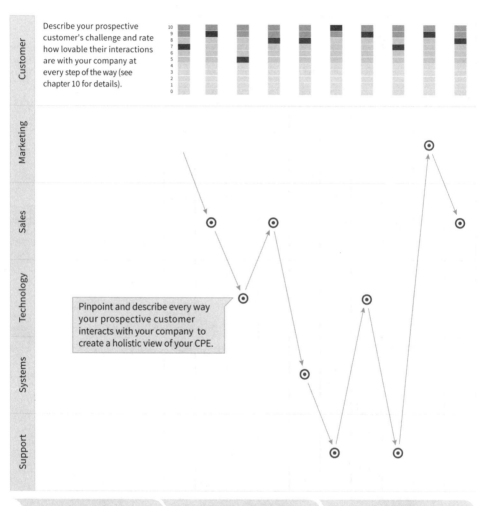

Describe your prospective customer's challenge and rate how lovable their interactions are with your company at every step of the way (see chapter 10 for details).

Pinpoint and describe every way your prospective customer interacts with your company to create a holistic view of your CPE.

Customer

Marketing

Sales

Technology

Systems

Support

Motivation

The problem and reasons your prospective customer has for seeking you out and the potential needs your product can satisfy.

Education

The prospective customer chooses from among a wealth of possible options for learning about your products and your company.

Adoption

The final experiences that convince a prospective customer to buy and those that frustrate them — leading them to give up on you.

Seeing the Patterns

One of the goals of this book is to help you look at the concept of product through your customer's eyes and feel it through their heart. That is a challenge, not only because you may not be used to thinking about your product in those terms, but because your customer is not thinking about the CPE either. Also, we are rarely just like our customers. You probably do not share their background or problems, so it is harder for you to understand where they're coming from.

How, then, can you develop the deep understanding and empathy that are the cornerstones of a transformative CPE? By using customer journey mapping to see the patterns in your interactions with past customers and employing listening and empathy to benefit the new customer you just met.

Pattern recognition is the source code of a lovable CPE. When you map thousands of customer interactions, you begin to see patterns of behavior and concerns. This helps you better understand what new customers are likely to need and ask for based on previous interactions with similar customers. Recognizing patterns is where some companies get their almost-prescient ability to anticipate customer needs and solve problems before the customer knows he or she has them — something that inevitably leads to customer delight and love.

Take the example of Express Scripts, one of the largest pharmacy benefit management companies in North America. They use predictive analytics to identify patients who are likely to be noncompliant in taking their prescribed medications. Armed with this information, they can then arrange an intervention from a healthcare provider or, for home delivery patients, deliver a compliance device, such as a cap with a timer that reminds patients to take their medications. This kind of intervention can save millions of dollars and save lives.

Pattern-based thinking grounds you in the now while getting you thinking of the future. Based on your understanding of who the customer is and what they need, you can predict what they are likely to ask — or are afraid to ask. You can anticipate needs, predict their journey, and make it smoother.

Beware the "Data Only" Trap

To do this, you must obsess about your customers and spend a lot of time talking about what they do and why. With enough data, you can start to accurately predict what they will ask for next — and deliver it. However, beware the "data only" trap.

Data can tell you what a customer is searching for and what thousands or even millions of others like them are looking for, but it will not tell you *why* they are searching. And even if you have the ability to track and analyze what aspects of your product your customers use, it will not tell you *why* they are using them. Data alone will not help you delight customers or make them love you. Lovability is about knowing customers like family *and* having data. You need insight based on a real understanding of your customers' challenges and what kind of customer experience they would benefit from. Meet with them, ask them for their thoughts, and collect their ideas.

It's not a requirement to have "walked in your customer's shoes" in order to deliver a satisfying experience. We all know what it feels like to be understood. We all crave a partner who "gets us" and understands what makes us unique. That is a very human need, and learning how to satisfy it should be a centerpiece of every engagement you have with your customers, whether you are just like them or not.

However, empathy is easier if you have experienced the pain your customers have experienced. If you want to increase your odds of understanding what your customers want and why, hire people who are like them. That is the reason we only hire former product managers to work with customers who are also innovators and product builders — they do not need to guess what it's like to create a product strategy or prioritize what the team will build next. Aha! Customer Success team members have already walked a mile in the customer's shoes, so they have deep knowledge of their needs and how to meet them . . . sometimes without having to ask.

> "If you want to increase your odds of understanding what your customers want and why, hire people who are like them."

Your Values Are Your Product

The better you understand your customers the better you can serve them. That is common sense. Then why do so many companies fail to do it? I believe there are two main reasons. First, it is hard work that is never done. Second, their values are misaligned.

Hard work is self-explanatory. To understand your customers, you need to connect with them, listen to them, and continue both as long as you are in business. That takes time and resources some leaders would rather allocate elsewhere. As for values, companies talk a great deal about them but few understand what they really are. Values encompass everything we have been talking about — understanding your customers' journey, having empathy for them, learning why they need what they need — and drive what's unique about your CPE. They make your product uniquely yours. If pattern recognition is your organization's source code, values are its operating system, running unseen under the surface but determining every action and outcome.

Values are answers to questions. What does your product represent? What does your company stand for? What will you always do and never do? What do you care about? Those answers determine how your people, from the founders to the newest hire, handle every situation, especially when they have to make a choice between what is convenient for the company and best for the customer. Values are a fail-safe for your corporate culture because when they are strong and widespread, they make harmful or self-serving decisions nearly impossible. They are your true north.

Your principles are your true north because they instruct how you will handle every situation, especially when there is no easy choice. Values begin with leadership and flow downstream to everyone else in the organization.

So, CEOs and product leaders, these questions are for you:

- What is the purpose of your product?
- What do you want your CPE to represent?
- What is the essence of your brand?

Let's talk about that word "brand" for a minute, since it's the first time we have brought it up. Corporate executives and marketers talk about brand even more than values, but as with values I am not sure that everybody is clear on what they are discussing. Your brand is an *outcome* — a result of your values playing out in the experiences of your customers. Your values drive your decisions and daily interactions. Those — not packaging or marketing — tell customers what you care about and stand for.

Your customers determine your brand. You can green-light all the expensive advertising initiatives you want, but a business is like a novelist or chef — the people who consume what you create decide if you are great. It is not enough to post your values on your website. In business, value is a verb. What matters is how the people who work for your company interpret your values and put them into action. That determines whether or not you have a brand that customers love. Your brand is what customers think and feel about your company, and it hinges on your CPE and whether you are reinforcing positive feelings and perceptions at every touch point.

The Aha! brand centers on the promise that we will respond with unheard-of speed to customer needs and make every interaction a breath of fresh air: caring, transparent, positive, and generous. That's strange for a software company, I know. But it's how we give our customers *mojo*. They expect that from us. That is the expression of our values. For example, if a customer tells us about a problem with our software, we love leaving them in disbelief when we respond 10 minutes later to tell them that we fixed it. It's even better when we reach out to them to say, "You did not know that you had this problem, but you did . . . and we just fixed it." It blows people's minds that a company could have their best interest in mind and act on it.

That sense that we know our customers better than they know themselves is our secret ingredient. We have world-class technology, but lots of companies are creating masterpieces with ones and zeroes. What sets companies like ours apart is that our values drive the CPE. Our values *are* our product.

Steven Kaplan, Senior Product Manager for LinkedIn, said about us, "Today everything runs out of Aha! — from product feedback to tracking progress on current features to sharing roadmaps. I know nothing is falling through the cracks and can spend more time doing what I love — dreaming up and building exciting new features." Or this from Bank of New Zealand, one of the country's largest banks: "It's like Aha! knew exactly what we needed before we knew we needed it."

The only way to get inside your customer's businesses — into their lives — and make that kind of real, positive difference is to know them and honestly care about helping them. Donna Sawyer, a team leader on our Customer Success team, said it perfectly:

> Nobody wants to be alone in their struggles. Customer service has barely changed over the years. It's been a place where you hire mostly inexperienced people and give them call scripts. They do their best to fix a problem. It's transactional at best. But real support for sophisticated customers should be mindful. The customer might be asking one question, but it's not really the question that will solve their problem. In the world of Customer Success, you must understand *why* the customer is asking what they are. If you do, you can provide the answer that they really need.

Product with a Purpose

At the heart of this conversation is something most corporate leaders do not spare a lot of thought for: *purpose.* So, let me ask again. What is the purpose of your product? It is not "to make money." Profit is the *outcome* of a well-executed CPE, not its purpose. Nobody asks what a product's purpose is — the product is seen as an end unto itself. But it is not that simple.

Not only can a product have a purpose, a lovable product *must* have one. Without purpose, your product is nothing more than a collection of atoms or bits. If your product is that shallow, your customer relationships will be, too. My experience has taught me this: The purpose of a product is to help customers achieve something meaningful in a lasting way.

That "something" will be different for each person, but the specifics do not matter. The best products empower each person who uses them to find meaning in their use, regardless of where the person is on their journey. The best products make us successful, better than we were before we found them. They give us a sense of relief that someone knows what we need, and they leave us believing that we received more value than what we paid. They leave us feeling happy and trusting that that feeling will never go away.

Can you think of at least one product in your life that has made you feel that way? Now, think beyond the product, the website or application or the object you hold in your hand. Have you ever had a CPE that has made you feel that way? Hold on to that feeling, because that is what you are striving for.

People will contact you to buy your product because they are looking to you to help them solve a problem and meet a need. That is probably the limit of their thinking. Great businesses have a greater purpose that their customers rarely ask for but always want — to make things better and better and better. Get to know them better than they know themselves and interact with them with urgency. Your customers have a problem that they need you to help solve — right now. If you solve it in ways they did not even know they cared about, they will love you for it for years, even decades.

Patterns, values, and purpose are the nucleic acids in the DNA of the CPE. Understanding your customers' journey, obsessing over what drives them, acting on a clear set of values, and constantly refining your CPE is the price of admission if you want to turn that DNA into products — and a company — that your customers love.

WORDS TO LOVE BY

- **Bits or atoms are not your product**
  Your product — what your customers are paying for and what will earn their loyalty and love — is the totality of their experiences with your people and your organization. That is the Complete Product Experience (CPE).

- **Your deliverable is a lovable CPE**
  The seven components of the CPE are: marketing, sales, technology, supporting systems, third-party integrations, support, and policies.

- **Service and relationships matter**
  These are the most powerful differentiators in your arsenal and your chief competitive edge. Particularly in the technology world, customers have a myriad of choices and products are often commodities.

- **Consider the customer journey**
  Customer journey mapping is an effective way to gain a greater understanding of your customers' experience with your company — what motivates them, how they need to be educated to continue to progress towards a purchase, and what they need to make the decision to adopt your solution.

- **Pattern recognition**
  Not only will pattern recognition help you provide customers with a better CPE, you can also use your experiences with past customers to predict the needs of future customers. The more customers you work with and the more deeply you understand what drives them and why, the more clearly you will see the patterns in their behavior.

- **Your values are your product**

  Your values are what you stand for. And no one can tell you what they are but you. Ask yourself: *What is the purpose of my product? What do I want my CPE to represent? And what is the essence of my brand?* And then go look and see if your actions are consistent with what you think you value.

- **Every product has a purpose**

  That purpose is to help the people who use it achieve something that is meaningful to them in a lasting way. Fulfilling that purpose should be every company's guiding star.

♡ *Chapter Two*

PURSUING LOVE

This is not just for the technocrats among us. Customer love is within reach for anyone who designs, builds, and delivers a product. Let me repeat that — anyone. These concepts are not complicated, with one caveat: You have to be willing to think differently about what you think you know about products and business and what can be loved.

Take Airbnb, one of the fastest-growing companies in the "sharing economy." The privately held peer-to-peer lodging marketplace posted revenues of nearly $1 billion in 2015,[1] has a valuation of approximately $30 billion, and boasts more than 2 million listings in more than 190 countries. But what makes Airbnb truly unique in a world of wannabes is its understanding that its product is not rooms (or even castles) for rent. It's trust. Hosts must trust that the company will screen members and ensure the integrity of their properties. Guests must trust that rentals are truthfully represented and that they will be physically safe. Both must trust that Airbnb will step up if things go sideways. Without trust, you may as well stay at a hotel.

Airbnb is delivering that trust. It is regularly in the top of most desired employers lists. It employs "scenario planning" to create immediate action plans for a range of incidents both plausible and implausible. (House party, anyone?) It even has a Trust and Safety Department dedicated to protecting the interests of all parties. Co-founder Brian Chesky summed it up when he said this:

> Probably the most important single piece of advice that I got — which is probably the most important advice I can give — [Paul Graham] basically drew out this chart and said "It's better to have 100 customers [who] love you than a million customers [who] just sort of love you." In other words, if you have 100 people [who] absolutely love your product they will tell 100 people, and then they will tell 100 people or even 10 people — and then this thing will grow.
>
> The problem is in Silicon Valley the general wisdom is "I need to build some app — this thing — and it needs to have this viral coefficient and I need to get millions of people to use it and they need to like it enough to share it." That's totally the wrong way of thinking about it. And so we literally decided: Do things, don't scale. It turns out getting 100 people [to] love you is really hard. It's easy to get 100 people to like you. To get them to love you, you need to meet them, you need to understand their problem.[2]

Six Traps of Innovation

Sounds simple. Deliver a product that makes customers love your company and let growth take care of itself. However, while everyone says they want the kind of fierce customer loyalty that turns into sustained profit, the operators of both startups and established, larger companies do not seem willing to do what is necessary to create it. Instead, they typically fall into one of six traps.

Six Traps of Innovation

There are many traps that innovators fall into. These are the most common ways that we have seen entrepreneurs struggle.

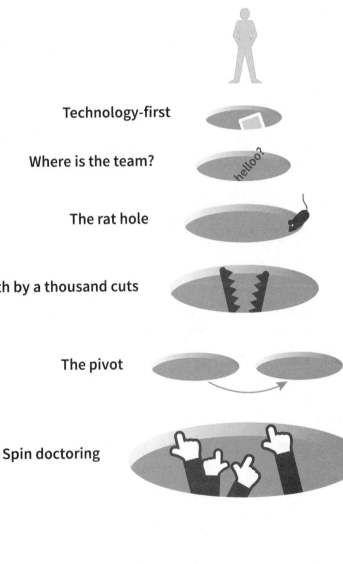

Technology-first

Where is the team?

The rat hole

Death by a thousand cuts

The pivot

Spin doctoring

Trap 1: Technology-first

These innovators know technology, but they are so focused on software or hardware as the solution to everything that they struggle to deeply understand who their customers are or how to provide them with an exceptional Complete Product Experience (CPE). This is commonly found in highly technical organizations where breakthrough technology is the goal rather than a means to deliver customer value.

Trap 2: Where is the team?

These innovators know the customer, but they do not have the product and technology teams in place to deliver what is needed. My experience is that consulting organizations that are trying to productize a methodology or custom software development project often fall into this trap. Building one product that serves many customers and has repeatable processes is significantly different than delivering custom, one-off solutions.

Trap 3: The rat hole

These innovators know technology and customers and know that they are supposed to be creating love, but they forget to start with clear goals. This makes every tunnel look like the right path toward success. Which of course is not true, because most are nothing but a dark dead end. They pursue so many different directions and spend so much time wandering that they never prioritize what matters most. This defines many startups I know.

Trap 4: Death by a thousand cuts

These innovators know they need to make progress, but they are paralyzed by infighting, fear, or a lack of strategy. So every new opportunity is considered with skepticism and shut down because it challenges the status quo. There are so many things that could go wrong when you try something new. And no one ever got promoted for being a failure. This paralysis is common in organizations that lack a clear purpose and others with an anxious culture that fears change. It is also more common in larger, established organizations than emerging companies.

Trap 5: The pivot

These innovators believe that at some critical moment, when a product fails, they can simply pivot their way to customer delight. The challenge is distinguishing between an idea that has no future and an idea that you have just not executed properly. Companies that cannot tell the difference often end up holding on to bad ideas too long and giving up on good ideas too early. Because it's fashionable, even suggested, to pivot when things go south, the consequences of being repeatedly wrong are understated. Unfortunately, failing fast can be habit-forming.

Trap 6: Spin doctoring

These innovators fall into the Indiana Jones boulder cave of traps: scary and hard to escape. Spin doctors know they want customer love but find it easier to focus on the perception that they are delivering it instead of making it so. Many well-funded startups fall into this category. They heavily hype their products and then the results disappoint. Expectations are high but unrealistic, and there is a lot of finger-pointing when things go wrong.

How Not to Build Product

No entrepreneur sets out to fall into any of these traps. We all set out to build something remarkable that will create value, help a lot of people become prosperous, and perhaps change a small part of the world. Unfortunately, even though we might start with the best of intentions, the prevailing "get big unnaturally fast" mentality leads too many talented and well-meaning people to fall into these traps.

The journey to the edge of the traps and to a painful fall is often down a path with four stages:

Stage one

You have an idea and have some experience in the market you are about to enter. You are either an engineer or you team up with one to build a prototype. You put together Microsoft PowerPoint presentations and set out to raise seed capital.

Stage two

Because you know someone, or your idea seems compelling on paper, you secure a few meetings with venture capitalists (VCs) or get invited to participate in a startup "demo day." Maybe some early customer traction helps validate your claim, and — wonder of wonders — there is interest in your idea.

Now you are caught. Meaningful investors want to fund businesses that can generate $100 million in revenue in five to seven years. How on earth are you going to make that happen? However, you are *so* close to funding your dream that you start bending the truth and exaggerating what is likely or even possible.

Stage three

You begin building market size models. In order to make the case that growing to $100 million is a possibility, those models need to get big fast. You find a few friendly customers to acknowledge that you are onto something and a few early adopters to commit to buying the first version of your product. You build marketing plans and customer acquisition models and someone says, "We'll fund it." You start to scale your team now that you are flush with cash, but from Day One you have a cloud over your head: The pressure of what you have promised.

How Not to Build a Product

Beware the product death spiral — big ideas should not be
immediately followed by big money.

Stage one — New product idea

Stage two — Seek venture capital

Stage three — Raise venture capital
based on big promises

Stage four — Rush to market with
an inferior product

Go back to Stage one until
you run out of ideas or money

Stage four

Desperation provokes compromise and bad behavior. You rush to market because you are told that you can iterate and even pivot if you need to. You try to add customers at any cost. This breeds internal strain when it proves to be harder than anyone thought. With investors looking over your shoulder, you do not have the time to build a superlative product so you manage perceptions instead. Cash starts to dry up. Pressure mounts. You must show traction or you will not be able to raise more money — or if you do, it will not be at the valuation you expect.

These are symptoms of "Jenga Syndrome" (inspired by the scene from *The Big Short* where Ryan Gosling uses Jenga blocks to explain the fragility of the credit default swaps market). The upper blocks are the market size, your revenue projections, and valuation — the things everybody gets excited about. But no matter how high you stack them, if you do not have a meaningful product and a rock-solid foundation of customer value at the base, the entire stack will inevitably crash.

This is my experience of what happens when things go really sideways. It is not every failed company's story, but I have seen it too many times to avoid warning you how not to build a product.

Please do not get me wrong. Venture capital is a critical component of the startup ecosystem. It provides many high-risk companies that do not have access to traditional financing a way to jump-start their business. Even the most efficient businesses need some capital to develop their products and companies. Without venture capitalists, many great companies would have never been created.

Investing in any company is a risky proposition, and that risk is exaggerated when a product and company is unproven. So, it is understandable that investors want to see a big future and have a say in the direction of the company. And it is totally reasonable that they press for a big return from a select few promising portfolio companies to make up for all the ones that fall into a trap or spiral out of control.

Remember that the product that venture capitalists sell to their own customers (the people and institutions who give them money to invest) is a financial gain. Their customers love them when those investments make them money. And they love it more when they make lots of money. That mindset is not always aligned with why entrepreneurs build companies.

Regardless, for many companies, raising money is a key part of their own adventure because their businesses are capital-intensive or they do not have access to other means to pursue their vision. However, when there is a disconnect between the reality of the financial future for a fresh new product and business and what is promised to investors, problems follow.

Home-Run Mentality

Let's imagine you avoid the traps, raise capital, and escape the product death spiral. Congratulations. You are on your way but must be vigilant to avoid another dangerous line of thinking — scale before profit and growth at all costs. You did not necessarily create this view of the world, but you are now a part of it. Once you accept an investment, you are no longer working just for yourself, your customers, and your employees.

The growing debris field of failed startups is collateral damage of the venture capital world's home-run mentality. Because venture investors' *raison d'être* is to find the next unicorn, their interests and those of entrepreneurs rarely align. Despite CB Insights findings that of more than 19,000 startups that raised angel, seed, or Series A funds between 2008 and 2014, fewer than one-half of 1 percent reached a billion-dollar valuation,[3] too many investors refuse to accept that the unicorn is a mythical creature. Instead, they try to improve their odds by throwing money at numerous companies in the hope that one will pay off handsomely.

But sometimes they get it right. And sometimes scale before profit is a reasonable path forward. Consider that some companies require massive infrastructure to be built to support their CPE. They need that infrastructure before they can deliver a lovable product.

Therefore, they require major infusions of cash to get going and continue to operate. Think about what it takes to build a data center or deploy a large fleet of cars. But these examples are the exception. They are very high-risk/ return scenarios that consume eye-popping amounts of cash and require founders to drive both the strategy and execution and continuously raise more money to feed the money-hungry operations. And they need leaders and investors with short memories and long-term outlooks.

Trying to get big fast tends to have the opposite effect, according to Fred Wilson of Union Square Ventures. Referencing data he "stares at all the time,"[4] Wilson noted that the amount of money raised by startups in their seed and Series A rounds is inversely correlated with success. You read that right — less money means more success.

> "The growing debris field of failed startups is collateral damage of the venture capital world's home-run mentality."

There are other doubtful views of the value of venture capital. When startups are raising money before they have traction, investors often require onerous terms to protect the perceived "market risk." While the terms may be tough for entrepreneurs to swallow, the trickle-down effect for shareholders can be even worse.

Connect Ventures founder Bill Earner even suggests that a build-value-first approach will lead to better investors later. In fact, it's part of how his firm evaluates potential investments. "We look for some form of engagement . . . There is some group of people that really really loves the product or service that the entrepreneur is making, and there is some proof of that," he told attendees at Capital On Stage, a venture capital conference. "Those are the things that are important to us."[5]

The question is not if or when you take other people's money; the question is what expectations do you set and what do you do with the money if you do take it. The reality is that nearly every lovable company highlighted in this book has funded its operations at one point or another via outside investment. So it is not that venture capital and lovability are mutually exclusive.

Committing to a CPE and lovability might not be the most exciting approach to building a business, but it is capital-efficient and minimizes pivots and rework along the way. And that is why, whether you are self-funding your business or leveraging third-party investments, pursuing lovability creates a competitive advantage for all.

Building on Love

From the beginning we wanted to build Aha! according to our own values. The home-run approach frequently leads to businesses that are miserable places for customers and employees alike. Obsessed with building valuation and pursuing the next round of funding, founders often delay focusing on the CPE, building customer value, or helping employees grow. Worse, by the time their ideas flourish and create value, founding team members own little or none of the company they started and have been replaced or moved on to pursue other opportunities.

We wanted to build something that real people with real needs would find value in and pay for. That was why we self-funded the company and never offered the service for free. Our only goal was to turn our vision into value for our customers, ourselves, and eventually for any employees we hired. Company valuation was not even part of our vocabulary.

That focus paid off fast. Through experience, customer devotion, hard work, and some good fortune we built a product that customers really wanted. And after a few months we noticed a pattern. Again and again, customers were using the word *love* to describe both our product and their experience when they needed help from us. Something extraordinary was happening — we were touching people, not just professionally but personally, inspiring an intense passion and loyalty that we had not expected. We named that quality *lovability*.

When we look back — not only at Aha! but at dozens of other business success stories — it is obvious that lovability is the only metric of success that really matters. If your customers love you, they will not only remain fiercely loyal but become your most powerful marketing asset. Lovability is the greatest predictor of business success. So, what is lovability?

Lovability is an inspirational state in which your Complete Product Experience (CPE) exceeds expectations to such an extent that your customers feel deep affection for what you provide them and actively work to contribute to your long-term success.

Lovability restores the customer to their proper place in the business hierarchy as the reason we are in business. It is the most important organizational metric, because customer love runs downstream to create loyalty, retention, profitability, and growth. Setting your target on lovability also simplifies decision-making. When faced with a choice, you simply ask, "Does this make our product and company more lovable?" If it does, proceed. If not, think twice.

> "If your customers love you, they will not only remain fiercely loyal but become your most powerful marketing asset."

What Lovability Looks Like

Lovability is something you earn. With lovable products, that begins with satisfying four fundamental needs. First, *utility*. A lovable product solves a real need. Think about the products you love. Would you feel the same if they did not help you achieve something important or complete meaningful tasks in a way that made your work better or your life easier?

Second, a lovable product meets and exceeds customer *expectations*. That is tough, because after years of overheated marketing, half-baked products, and service horrors, customers expect to be disappointed. But they are always hopeful that the next product or company will be the one that dazzles them. If it is yours, these customers will keep coming back and telling their colleagues and friends.

Long-term loyalty equals profit. In their 2015 *Ecommerce Growth* benchmark report, RJMetrics found that past year three of operation, the most successful e-commerce businesses earned the majority of their revenues from repeat customers.[6]

On a personal note, I once bought a pair of hiking boots from REI and wore them around for a few weeks to break them in. But they ended up destroying my feet on a backpacking trip to Emigrant Wilderness in the Sierra Nevada mountains in California. When I returned home, I hobbled back to the store to return them, fearing the company would refuse. But REI did not hesitate to give me my money back, and in doing so they further solidified my love and loyalty. I continue to buy equipment and clothing at REI with confidence that they will always treat me well when something does not work out.

Third, lovability is backed with *integrity* — earnest people doing the right thing even when it would be easier not to. Love is not a transaction. It is a relationship refreshed and strengthened over time by valuable interactions. Enduring relationships thrive on mutual respect and customers' belief that a business puts their interests first. Your customers should know what you believe in and trust that you will stay true to those core principles.

In the classic book *How Will You Measure Your Life?*, co-authors Clayton M. Christensen, James Allworth, and Karen Dillon frame the issue in starker terms, pointing out that it is easier to stay true to your principles 100 percent of the time than it is to hold steady 98 percent of the time. According to the authors, your personal moral line is powerful because you do not cross it. But once you do, no matter your justifications, you are more likely to do it again.[7]

In other words, do the right thing because it's the right thing. That's especially challenging in emerging organizations where people are under pressure to rapidly grow the business. But when delivering a CPE is your focus, it is easy to see why doing the right thing is so important. Operating with integrity depends on the entire team, so the actions of each person matter. Every person faces situations where they need to put customers' or colleagues' interests ahead of their own, and their decisions reflect the organization's core values. What do your choices — and your team's choices — say about your values?

We are not saints at Aha! We make mistakes, misunderstand customers, and sometimes even hire people who are not a great fit and end up moving on. But we work daily to ensure that our people reflect our values and act with integrity. For example, we encourage people to write the word "NO" on a sticky note and put it on their computers to remind them that it is okay to say no to a customer or anyone else who asks them to compromise our principles.

That pays dividends. Recently, a member of our Customer Success team was put in a position where she would have had to lie to a customer. She said, "I just don't feel right about this." We immediately changed company policy due to her rightful concern.

In some organizations, she would have been ignored or told, "Who cares? Get the money!" Integrity means building an environment where people not only feel comfortable expressing moral or ethical concerns because they feel they'll be taken seriously, but where they *are* taken seriously and provoke meaningful change.

Finally, lovability is a *journey*. People change. Your organization changes. Your customers' needs change. As these changes occur, acknowledge that you may not be the right solution for everyone. Sometimes, caring about customers means telling them that you're not a good fit — and even helping them find an alternative.

In a lovable company, employees are growing, too. Employees who are challenged and growing are passionate about being their best. That translates into every interaction and everything they do.

In a lovable company that focuses on the CPE, employees are expected to have a positive impact on their customers and team no matter what their title is. That mindset helps every employee feel connected to the higher purpose of the business and understand how they are contributing to its success. A company can only keep delivering a CPE that its customers love if its employees love the company, too.

"Lovability is a journey. People change. Your organization changes. Your customers' needs change."

WORDS TO LOVE BY

- **Six traps of innovation**
  Building a lovable product is hard. Really hard. Entrepreneurs should avoid six common traps that are difficult to climb out of once you fall into one or stumble into another, including the rat hole and the pivot.

- **Other people's money**
  The common approach to building a product, especially a technology product, starts with a bold idea. It is typically followed by seeking outside investment before creating real customer value. Building organically by first creating real value for real people is a proven, sustainable alternative whether you ever raise funds or not.

- **"Jenga Syndrome" is a real danger**
  It refers to the vulnerability of a business that builds valuation and brand on the basis of hype, not legitimate customer value. Without a foundation of genuine customer value, the collapse of a business is inevitable.

- **Lovability is an inspirational state**
  It is inspirational in the sense that your Complete Product Experience (CPE) exceeds expectations to such an extent that your customers feel deep affection for what you provide them and work to actively contribute to your long-term success. It is the most important organizational metric, because customer love runs downstream to create loyalty, retention, profitability, and growth.

- **Lovability must be the linchpin of all decisions**
  Simply asking "Will this make our product and company more lovable?" is a simple, effective decision-making heuristic for any department, from sales and marketing to engineering and customer support.

- **Lovability hinges on three qualities**
  First, utility. Your product has to be useful and solve a problem. Second, your CPE must consistently exceed customer expectations. Third, your people and organization must act with integrity and reflect authentic, consistent values.

- **Lovability is also a journey**
  Your company will change. Your people will change. Your products and the customers who use them will change. You may not always be the right solution for everyone, so being lovable also means letting customers go when they can go elsewhere to find greater value. At the end of the day, lovability means having a positive impact on everyone who comes into contact with your organization.

Chapter Three

THE TEN BUILDING BLOCKS OF LOVABILITY

In the last chapter of this book, I will introduce you to tools you can use to assess your company's lovability and help build the kind of love I have described. That is what your customers want, even if they cannot express it that way. But first, let's look at the building blocks that make lovability possible.

The building blocks appear roughly in sequence in three stages of your customer's product adoption process. As the stages progress, each building block becomes harder to achieve yet more important to lovability. By gauging how many building blocks your business is delivering, you can get an accurate picture of what you need to earn customer love and loyalty.

Every person in an organization has a role to play in building a lovable product. But for product leaders and executives, this is where you can be difference makers. You are well-positioned to see the entire customer experience and where your company is falling short. You have the power to do what is necessary to create purpose and course-correct as necessary.

Stage One: Utility

The must-haves. Without them, you do not have a customer.

1. Hope

Customer sentiment: "Finally, something that looks like it will solve my problem!"

The customer has been looking for a solution — possibly without even knowing what to search for — and your marketing or word of mouth has led them to you. That is a start. This is the first and most generic part of lovability. The customer has not used your product yet and is simply hoping that it will solve their most basic need.

2. Satisfaction

Customer sentiment: "I tried it and it actually does make my life better. I can take a breath now."

Marketing has created an expectation. Now the Complete Product Experience (CPE) must deliver a reality that makes the customer smile. If you deliver on the promise to meet the customer's need, that is the true beginning point of the CPE. However, satisfaction is experience-specific and precarious. Your solution must deliver as promised every time in this early stage, or your relationship with that customer may end before it can begin.

3. Care

Customer sentiment: "I get the help I need to get the most from the product."

This is a crucial transition point. Without a CPE philosophy as your foundation, you will not create customer value or be responsive. You will never get past Utility.

Treat the trial, purchase, and initial use of your product — a transaction that might take days, hours, or even minutes — as just the tip of the iceberg that is your product. Your CPE, which could support a relationship that could last for years, is the other 90 percent of the iceberg — the part that lies below the water and it is anchored by customer support (or as we call our team at Aha! — Customer Success).

Delivering lovable support should be simple — the bar is set low. However, businesses swim upstream against a current of negative stereotypes. Customers get stuck in interactive voice response systems, nobody understands the advanced features of the product, and so on. Lovability means going the extra mile to counter skepticism and provide a CPE that blows past expectations.

It is a binary situation: Defy expectations of poor service and create customer delight or live down to them and validate customer frustration. Apple's Genius Bar is a perfect example of support that adds value and enhances the customer relationship. Apple brings you into an environment that perfectly reflects the brand and then hands you over to an expert who not only solves your problem but also might teach you something about the product that you did not know.

At the other extreme is my experience with Enterprise Rent-A-Car. I needed to rent a car for a trip to Scotland, and while I used the Enterprise website, the support center representative was responsible for delivering the CPE. She failed. She could not tell me whether someone in the United States could rent cars through the U.K. website (they can) and did not recognize the name of Glasgow, the biggest city in Scotland. Enterprise couldn't even get past Hope.

That does not happen by accident. It happens because people do not care. It happens when the leaders in the organization or the people doing the day-to-day customer support work become apathetic. As Barry Schwartz pointed out in *Why We Work*, if you do not have a good reason why you do what you do, you will not care about doing it well or making a difference.[1]

Stage Two: Growth

A meaningful partnership between company and customers starts to emerge.

4. Confidence

Customer sentiment: "I know the company will be there for me."
The customer is certain that the product will deliver value as promised and be there for them when they need it. They also have a sense of safety and security about the company itself. They believe that when something goes wrong or there is a question they cannot answer, there will be someone on the other end of the phone who can help.

5. Trust

Customer sentiment: "The company and its people care about me."
The gap between Confidence and Trust is small but vital. With Trust, customers believe not only in the hardware or software they use, but in the CPE. They believe in your people, values, and mission. You have done it — built a relationship where your customers have faith that you are concerned with their welfare and will be there for them when the chips are down.

Trust grows from "moments of truth" when you have to back up your values with action. My co-founder, Chris Waters, explains how Aha! handles such moments in the form of software bugs: "When a customer reports a bug, we drop everything to solve it straightaway. We do this for a number of reasons. First, we want to make the customer happy and help them get back to the important work they are doing. More importantly, if one customer is reporting a problem, we can only assume there are dozens or hundreds more who did not report it. That's why we never underestimate even the most trivial bug. If we did what most engineering teams do — capture bug reports, file them, and fix them when the schedule allows — who knows how many other thousands of users would stumble across the bug in the meantime and be unhappy?"

> "If one customer is reporting a problem, assume there are a hundred more who did not report it. Never underestimate even the most trivial bug."

Attacking bugs immediately helps us avoid "technical debt," which occurs when you delay fixing problems for so long that it becomes impossible (or prohibitively expensive) to catch up. Above all, solving problems builds trust. Trust grows when your values, goals, and aspirations align with those of your customers. If your people's behavior reflects your authentic values, customers will begin to view you not as a service provider but as a trusted partner. That is when love begins.

The Lovability Line

This is *The Lovability Line*, the point where customers start judging your company less on rational criteria and more on emotional ones. From here on, they become more emotionally invested in what you do and how you do it. It is up to you to sustain that love by adhering to your values and continuing to deliver an extraordinary CPE.

6. Scale

Customer sentiment: "As I get better, the product already has what I need." Customers use words like "magic" to describe this. Your product is always slightly out in front of customer needs and expectations. With a complex product like a software application or a smartphone, new users generally use only a fraction of the functionality because they have a specific problem in mind.

As time goes by, however, users have new needs that require new functionality. A company that is committed to delivering a CPE anticipates those needs and builds in the additional functionality before it's needed. It seems like the product knows where you are going and has what you need waiting for you when you arrive. Nothing else creates such delight. At Aha!, when customers tell us, "Every time I go to do something new, the software does it for me," they are experiencing that delight. Scale is the "wow factor" that wins customers for life and creates the world's most valuable brands.

7. Sustainability

Customer sentiment: "The people and processes that deliver my experience will be there in the future."

Customers trust that your company will be there a year from now and five years from now, still providing the same lovable CPE. Your culture, attention to detail, desire for excellence, commitment to people, and innovative spirit ensure continuity for customers. They also feel secure that you will not allow the company to turn into something unrecognizable.

> "Your culture, attention to detail, desire for excellence, commitment to people, and innovative spirit ensure continuity for customers."

That's counter to the prevailing approach in high-tech — build fast, exploit what you can, get out, and get rich. Customers? They're the next owner's problem. Lovability is the antidote to that thinking.

Wait, what about the two traditionally funded startups Chris and I built that were acquired by well-known, public technology companies in four years? Yes, but acquisition was never our aim. We are "optimistic realists." For an optimistic realist, it is possible to build for long-term, sustainable happiness and then decide that you might not achieve that by holding on to what you have built. And sometimes, as we have learned when you have investors, you are not fully in control of your future. So selling your business is always a possibility, and when you do it at the right time and for the right reasons, it creates more value than continuing to build on your own. While you must plan for long-term success, it is possible to set what you love free, continue to deliver on your promise to customers, and still prosper.

Stage Three: Inspiration

Love, passion, and obsessive fandom arise. Movements follow.

8. Motivation

Customer sentiment: "I'm better than I was before this product and it will make me even better tomorrow."

Customers feel that the product helps them be better than they are without it. Maybe it gives them information or capabilities they did not have before. Or it gives them feedback that inspires them to work harder, learn more, or push themselves.

I am a cyclist, and I use the Strava mobile app — an activity tracker with built-in GPS and a social network for athletes — both to record my speed and routes on rides and connect with other cyclists. That real-time data not only provides a history of what I have accomplished each year, but also lets me compare my times to others, inspiring me to push myself just a bit more the next time.

9. Fun

Customer sentiment: "I have a good time using the product."

This is less about being passively entertained and more about helping people achieve what they care about most and enjoy the process. It's about making them smile on their journey to success, even when they are working really hard to get there. The best products help customers be better at what they love to do and make the less desirable aspects of their work easier to tolerate. They are aspirational.

Take the Pokémon Go craze. It might seem silly to chase after digital monsters in an augmented reality environment on your phone, but a lot of players reported that while doing so they were getting more exercise than they had in years. They did not set out to be healthier or lose weight, but the app helped them do it anyway and have fun in the process. No wonder it was the fastest game to reach number one on mobile revenue charts.[2]

10. Halo

Customer sentiment: "The product makes me look really, really good."

We're social animals, and we love to be recognized for our activity and achievement. If your product is built on the other nine building blocks and improves how others view your customer, you have found the pinnacle of profitability and sustainable happiness.

Visually, the building blocks stack up like this:

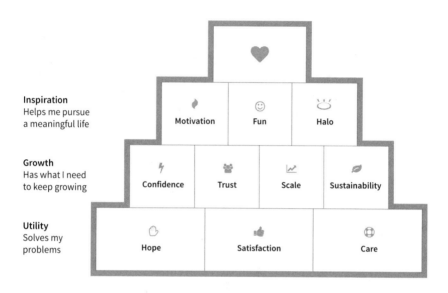

Inspiration
Helps me pursue
a meaningful life

Motivation   Fun   Halo

Growth
Has what I need
to keep growing

Confidence   Trust   Scale   Sustainability

Utility
Solves my
problems

Hope   Satisfaction   Care

The Three Signs of Lovability

When properly joined, the building blocks are the pillars of lovable products. However, when you are immersed in the daily demands of running a department or company, it can be hard to see whether you are stacking the blocks to create lovability or building a Jenga tower sure to collapse. Fortunately, just like romantic love, lovability has its telltale signs.

The first sign to look for is Hugs. Customers want to get closer to your product and your team because they feel connected to it. They feel affection and delight for your product and feel that it helps them do meaningful things. You will know because they will express strong emotions about your product and people. They want to pull you in closer so you can understand what they need from you to do meaningful work more efficiently.

Michel Besner saw this when he was CEO of Toon Boom Animation, a Montreal company that builds animation and storyboarding software for film and television producers. I asked him about how he connected with customers. "We had people on the road all the time, meeting with our customers," he told me. "They would visit production facilities and sound studios to see them in action and see the work they were doing. Toon Boom's customers are very passionate. They want to create great art and they will go to great lengths to make sure that we understand their needs. They really wanted us to understand them and their work so we could create better products for them."

You know you are getting Hugs when you see . . .

- Customers prioritizing their time to spend it with you or your products.
- Verbal expressions of admiration for your product. Customers tell you that your product is good, different, and that other companies would benefit from it.
- Customers insisting that you "get" them, their values, and what they care about.
- Customers spending political capital to recommend your product and company to others, even when it's over an established alternative.
- Customers telling you they want your product and team to succeed.
- Customers apply for open jobs at your company because they want to come work with you.

When your customers express these feelings, you have achieved lovability. That does not mean it will last, though. Business relationships, like friendships, take work.

The second sign is Love Notes. After customers get closer to your company and people and you continue to treat them with kindness, they will fall in love. And as people have done for centuries, they'll write notes sharing their feelings with the object of their affection. For Aha! those notes can be emails, social media posts, instant messages, referrals, or even customer satisfaction surveys, but they have a common message — heartfelt expressions of love for our people and our CPE. A sampling:

> *"Our CEO is actually doing most of the initial input and is absolutely 'In Love' with Aha already. His comment was that it's almost like you were listening to what he needed for the last five years and you implemented it. Seriously great work and a great product; we really don't know what we would have done if we didn't find Aha!"*

> *"Love your product. It is amazing, one of the best products I have seen in a long time."*

> *"By the way, kudos to your support team. I've had a number of questions during my evaluation of Aha! and everyone has been incredibly responsive and knowledgeable. Your support team has been the best salesman for you guys so far!"*

> *"I have to say I've introduced my team to Aha! in the past week and they are absolutely loving it. We are very much looking forward to becoming a customer."*

We were surprised by this at first, but now we actually measure the number of messages we get where customers tell us they love us. It is an operating metric that we track and report on quarterly. Nobody does that. It seems too simple and crude. However, it is the most holistic way to look at the success of what we are giving people. It's so simple that somebody coming out of business school might not even give it a second thought. But it works.

You could use customer growth as a metric, because if you are not doing something right, you will not get new customers. But there is not always a clear correlation between growth and love. A company with a monopoly-like position such as AT&T can grow even if their customers despise them. To wit: The telecommunications giant reported more than $42 billion in consolidated revenue in the fourth quarter of 2015,[3] yet regularly makes its way onto the list of most hated companies in America.[4] Love Notes are more reliable.

The final sign is Megaphones. Customers tell their friends and colleagues about how wonderful you are — and those people will tell *more* colleagues and friends. Since any paid advertising is regarded with increasing suspicion, word of mouth and unsolicited enthusiasm on social networks or review sites like Yelp are more influential than ever.

When Megaphones are in action, you'll find customers will find increasingly interesting ways to realize value from your product and the interactions they have with your company. Customers are more likely to adopt or even champion your solution again if they change companies — the ultimate expression of loyalty.

Lovability from the Ground Up

There is no magic to lovability. Anyone with the right mindset can build a lovable product. But building it requires the basic skills, the intrinsic motivation, and a purpose beyond mere growth.

Stay curious. To get to genuine lovability, keep digging and understand your customers' real needs and motivations. You must get not just what they're trying to do but the motivations behind their actions, and that means finding joy and meaning in helping them. It means loving them back.

Start with Utility, especially when your potential customer has a lot of pain or frustration. It does not matter how much fun your product is to use if it doesn't solve a problem and is not reliable. Aim for Relief, Satisfaction, Support, Confidence, and Trust. To have a chance to build something extraordinary, you must at least step to the Lovability Line.

That leads us to the Law of Lovability:

The more building blocks of lovability your product delivers, the greater the odds that your customers will find it lovable.

If a company consistently experiences eight to 10 of the building blocks, you are earning intense customer love and loyalty. Think: Apple, Minecraft, REI, Southwest Airlines, and Tesla — brands with passionate, lifelong customers. Companies with five to seven building blocks can be loved, but the emotions will be volatile and changeable. This group includes companies like Facebook, Google, Salesforce, Slack, and Zillow. With fewer than five building blocks, lovability is impossible.

No matter where your organization is on the scale, lovability is neither static nor guaranteed. It takes purpose, commitment, and work to keep delivering a CPE and sustain that love. When you have it, you have earned it.

WORDS TO LOVE BY

Ten building blocks of lovability

Hope, Satisfaction, Care, Confidence, and Trust are your foundation. You cannot have lovability without them. Scale, Sustainability, Motivation, Fun, and Halo are required to earn the kind of passion and lifelong loyalty achieved by the world's top brands.

- **Hope**

  Stage one. Utility begins here. Your product represents the prayed-for end to the customer's long search for something, anything, that might solve their problem or meet their need. Marketing or word of mouth has led them to you, and before they have even used your product, they are hoping that it will fill their long-standing need.

- **Satisfaction**

  The customer has tried the product and it has delivered as promised. The customer is not in love yet, but they are happy that your product did what your marketing said it would. Satisfaction is transitory, however. In the early stages, your product needs to perform as advertised every time or the customer will quickly become disillusioned and look elsewhere.

- **Care**

  The Complete Product Experience (CPE) takes shape. This is where customer support steps up to elevate things from a mere transaction to a relationship between your company and the customer. Especially on the first occasion that the customer reaches out with a problem or a question, they should find an absolute commitment to being the solution and creating delight. For this to happen, there must be a strong, clear "why" behind the work you do.

- **Confidence**

  Stage two. Growth begins. A meaningful partnership between you and your customers starts to develop. Based on the performance of your product, a quality CPE, and your company keeping its promises, customers begin to be confident that your company will be there when they need you. In other words, they believe you have their back at all times. Trust has begun to form.

- **Trust**

  Customers are not just confident in what you do, they believe in who you are and that you stand for the values that you espouse. They have dropped any last cynicism and skepticism and really buy into who you say you are. This is the pivotal stage called *The Lovability Line*, where customers become more emotionally invested in your company and products and judge you less on empirical factors and more on emotional ones.

- **Scale**

  Customers are amazed that new versions of your product always seem to anticipate their future needs before they know what those needs will be. This is the "wow factor" that makes customers use words like "magic," wins loyalty, and leads to world-class brands.

- **Sustainability**

  Your culture, attention to detail, care for your team, and clear purpose behind your work breed longevity of your company and the people who create the lovable CPE. Customers trust that your company will be doing well a year from now and 10 years from now, still delivering quality products and a wonderful CPE. It's this quality that makes them comfortable committing to your cause 100 percent and also referring other individuals and businesses to you.

- **Motivation**

  Stage three. Inspiration begins here. Customers feel that your product makes them better than they were without it. Perhaps it gives them capabilities they would not have, helps them be more productive, or serves their creativity.

- **Fun**

  Your product helps your customers enjoy what they do more — whatever it is. This is less about pure fun — though there is nothing wrong with that — and more about helping people achieve what they truly care about and enjoy the journey. Your products help your customers breeze through the parts of their work that they love doing and make the less desirable parts more tolerable.

- **Halo**

  Using your products makes your customers look awesome in front of their peers, superiors, or friends.

Lovability shows itself in three ways

You receive Hugs when customers try to get physically close to your company and people. Love Notes can be anything from emails to tweets expressing customer affection, enthusiasm, and loyalty. And when they start using Megaphones — word of mouth, online reviews, referrals — lasting growth and sustainable happiness follows.

- **The first sign that you have achieved lovability is Hugs**

  Customers express feelings of affection for your product and want to get closer to it, your employees, and your company. Signs of Hugs include customers insisting that you "get" them and what they care about, customers spending political capital to recommend your products over an entrenched competitor, and customers wanting you, your team, and your company to succeed. You also see customers applying to join your team because they believe in the product and your purpose.

- **The second sign is Love Notes**
  Customers will send your company expressions of their delight with your people, products, and CPE. These can be via email, social media, review websites, instant messages, voice mail — virtually any means of saying, "Thanks for everything you do. I love you guys."

- **The third sign is Megaphones**
  Customers who love your CPE will tell friends and colleagues how wonderful you are, becoming your most powerful and effective marketers and advertisements. If they are business customers, they are also more likely to adopt your solution again if they change companies, which is the ultimate expression of loyalty.

♡ *Chapter Four*

THE BENEFITS OF BEING LOVED

Love is a fundamental concept central to all human interactions. It is a driver of good health and happiness. Business is made up of human interactions. Do the math and the solution is clear: Love is central to business. No longer should love be relevant only in the home, nor should it be a soft-squishy metric. Love is measurable, trackable, and predictable. It belongs in the workplace.

Companies that understand this take intentional, strategic, and consistent action to cultivate the building blocks of lovability, and it pays dividends. For example, UnitedHealth Group was named *Fortune's* "World's Most Admired Company" in Insurance and Managed Care for 2016 — its sixth consecutive year in the top spot.[1]

To learn how UnitedHealth Group has achieved such a consistently stellar reputation, I talked to Donna Sawyer, a team leader on the Aha! Customer Success team who you met in chapter 1. She is a customer of UnitedHealth Group's Optum healthcare technology unit and said of her experience:

> I lost my thyroid function a while back so I have a recurring pre-
> scription for life. We moved over to United Healthcare when I

joined Aha!, and Optum's partnership with United Healthcare is completely awesome. At signup, Optum asked if I wanted my recurring prescription auto-filled, and I said yes and entered my credit card information. They managed everything with my doctor: When I need a refill, they send it, bill my Health Reimbursement Account (HRA), and the HRA sends me a reimbursement check. It's hands-free. I always wasted time getting reimbursements and forgetting to refill, but not anymore.

For Donna, Optum hit all five essential building blocks below the Lovability Line. They have given her relief from a long-standing problem, delivered a satisfying experience, and offered support by working with her doctor, and they are a large company that will be around for a while. They have earned her trust and loyalty.

According to Art Swanson, Optum's Vice President of Product Management, Solutions and Technology, the company is not stopping there. I asked him about his goal to create something rarely seen in the healthcare space — delight:

> Healthcare is a dynamic space now and the way the system should work is still under construction. We're transitioning from fee-for-service to value-based care, no one knows how that is going to turn out. From an enterprise system perspective, we're still in "remove my pain" mode. We're not in a place where we can do delightful things yet. If you inject delightful experiences in the middle of a painful workflow, it can come across as disingenuous and actually make things worse. But once we have stability, we'll be able to be intentional about building delightful experiences for clinicians and patients.

Love Is in the Eye of the Beholder

The contrast between Donna's experience and Art's guarded perspective shows that creating lovability is never finished. There is always more an organization can do. However, even in a business sector where relationships are complex and turf battles common, you will always be better off taking action to anticipate your customers' needs and solve their problems, even if you do not have a comprehensive "love and delight" strategy in place yet. An unremarkable experience for one person could be one that wins undying allegiance for another.

How do you know? By tracking customer sentiment. Organizations can measure customer affection by tracking incoming messages that express love, loyalty, and enthusiasm. Determine where the bar is set for a message to count as a Love Note (can it say something like "You guys are the best company ever!" or does it need to be more specific?) and then follow how such messages increase or decrease. Patterns will emerge. Perhaps customer love rises during certain times of year and falls during others. Do you get less love after a software release but more when you release an update that fixes bugs? How does all this affect your overall lovability score? (In chapter 10, I will introduce you to several tools you can use to gauge lovability and assess how it changes over time.)

Some businesses take a unique approach to this. Footwear brand Toms, already beloved thanks to its renowned blend of "social purpose" and product, forgoes splashy celebrity marketing campaigns. Instead, they engage and elevate real customers. During the summer of 2016, Toms engaged more than 3.5 million people in a single day using what they call *tribe power*. The company tapped into its army of social media followers for its annual One Day Without Shoes initiative to gather millions of Love Notes on social media.

However, Toms U.K. marketing manager Sheela Thandasseri explained that their tribe's Love Notes are not relegated to one day. "Our customers create social content all the time showing them gifting Toms or wearing them on their wedding day, and they tag us because they want us to be part of it."[2]

Toms uses customer experience management platform Sprinklr to aggregate interactions on Facebook, Instagram, and Twitter. Toms then engages in a deep analysis of the data generated by its tribe, learning what customers relish and dislike about its products, stores, and salespeople so they can optimize their Complete Product Experience (CPE).

That is an aggressive, all-in approach that extracts as much data as possible from every customer interaction in order to see patterns and craft experiences. Your approach might differ based on factors ranging from budget limitations to privacy concerns. But I can attest that earning love does not necessarily require cutting-edge technology or huge expenditures. What it does require is a commitment to delivering the building blocks of lovability that I reviewed in the previous chapter. Lovability begins with a mindset that makes it a priority.

The building blocks are feelings — hope, confidence, fun. If you stack them up over and over again, eventually you will turn those feelings into a tower of meaningful benefits for everyone with a stake in your business, including owners, investors, employees, and customers. Now let's look more closely at those benefits and the groups they affect.

"Lovability begins with a mindset that makes it a priority."

How Lovability Benefits Customers

For customers, lovability is a consequence of policies and attitudes that bring tangible benefits. Your customers do not care about loving your company — their main concern is that your product solves their problems and makes their lives better. Love should not be an end in itself. If you catch yourself or employees saying, "We need to make our customers love us," go back to the drawing board. Love comes from providing extraordinary value, being responsive, and nurturing relationships.

For customers, lovability . . .

Solves a problem

Lovable products satisfy practical needs that customers have today. That might mean making their lives easier, saving them money, or saving them time. Think about how Optum's digital prescription solution benefits Donna. It frees her from calling her physician or pharmacist for refills, prevents her from running out of medication, and takes one thing off her to-do list. It makes her life more convenient and empowers her to better manage her time.

Then there's iRobot's Roomba automated vacuum. It has been around for a while and became a punchline in YouTube videos featuring cats, dogs, kids, and turtles chasing, riding, or otherwise abusing the thing. But it is also a perfect example of a product that works well and satisfies a basic need — keeping your house clean 24 hours a day so you do not have to worry about messes. Customers love the Roomba. When you go to its Amazon product page, one of the first reviews is headlined, "I am in love!" That is the kind of enthusiasm and unbridled passion any company should be looking to engender.

Means helpful, effective support personnel

In a lovable organization, customers find people who not only help but understand them. Customers love finding real, relatable people they can connect with on a personal basis while addressing any issues they may have. When that happens, they feel heard and cared for. You will hear customers and employees alike laughing and sharing stories when they interact, like they are talking to old friends.

When you nurture that kind of relationship at a time when someone is interested in buying your product or needs support, you are on your way. From the customer's perspective, the person on the other end of the phone or answering emails genuinely cares about making things better for them. If that means an upgrade or purchasing a new product, that is probably okay.

However, being relatable will only take you so far without responsive problem solving. The story about the support representative from managed hosting company Rackspace who sent a beleaguered customer pizza while on a lengthy call may have gone viral, but it is not why Rackspace has earned numerous awards for its "fanatical support." Customers might enjoy talking with someone who knows their purchase history and remembers their birthday, but they want someone who will help them. Rackspace employees go through an extensive training program, including learning about the company's history and core values, participating in exercises and games that teach them how to serve customers, role-playing to fine-tune their ability to resolve specific support situations, and taking a trip through the Strengths-Finder assessment tool to learn their five personal strengths and how to maximize them on the job.[3]

Businesses need to start listening to and delivering on what customers expect, according to Professor Mary Jo Bitner, co-executive director of the Center for Services Leadership at the W. P. Carey School of Business at Arizona State University, who helped design an annual "customer rage" survey. Of the 2015 survey, Bitner said, "Customer service is critical. Its success depends on truly understanding what customers expect, and then, even more importantly, delivering on those expectations. The companies that are doing it well regularly take the pulse of their markets and also have metrics to assess whether they are succeeding."[4]

Offers a meaningful future

When lovability is strong, customers feel like the product and company make them better at what they do today and inspire them to excel at even more meaningful work tomorrow. They are confident that your product will solve problems that they cannot even foresee. You are giving them serious mojo. This is a rare state that few businesses achieve. But it is achievable.

The takeaway: Lovability produces a lasting customer relationship that yields maximum value for both customer and business.

"Being relatable will only take you so far without responsive problem solving."

How Lovability Benefits Employees

Businesses with high lovability treat employees not only as vital parts of the mutual value equation but at least as equal to customers in importance. Customers may be the final arbiters of love, but employees are its agents, creating the CPE that earns love and loyalty. Organizations that earn love from their customers go beyond basic aspects of employee satisfaction like compensation to provide deeper, more meaningful benefits like . . .

A sense of purpose

Every company's purpose is to acquire customers. The best way to do that is to provide something meaningful to them. Lovable organizations prioritize building a CPE and strong customer relationships because they are the vehicle for creating meaning.

That became our center of gravity in building Aha! We were always product builders and therefore knew what other product builders — our customers — needed. We also knew how we liked to be treated by vendors and how infrequently that happened. We wanted to deliver a product that helped customers build their own solutions while making every customer touch point relational, not transactional. The high-pressure approach to selling that dominates in technology companies today forces people to arbitrate between their own interests and the customers' interests. We were determined to avoid that.

This relationship-first philosophy allows employees to approach their work with a higher purpose: Create value for the customer in every way possible. No hidden agendas. No suggestive selling. Employees have the luxury of dealing with customers in the same way *they* want to be dealt with when they are the customer — with integrity. That helps them feel good about what they do.

Focus on achievement

Products exist to help people achieve meaningful things, but customers are not the only ones who want to do that. Employees also crave achievement.

They want to get better at what they do, help people, learn new skills, and maybe even grow into starting the type of business they have always admired, like Chris and I did.

Lovable organizations do not ask employees to manage perceptions — a kinder way of saying "manipulating what people think versus optimizing what they experience." Instead, lovability lets employees focus on being better. That means honing their skills, learning new ones, setting and reaching loftier goals, and growing as human beings.

Sustainable happiness

Our ultimate goal is internal lovability. With sustainable happiness, employees love what they do, like the people with whom they do it, and know that the organization respects and appreciates them. Employee engagement is a hot-button topic right now, and these are the conditions that create engagement, where employees bring their heads, hands, and hearts to their work.

Sustainability comes from synergy between the personal and professional parts of each employee's life. This might surprise you, but I do not believe in "work-life balance." Balance is inherently precarious and crashes are inevitable. The Aha! way — growing customer relationships and being ultra-responsive — is hard work. Many of our employees tell us they are working harder than ever before but that they love it. That has nothing to do with balance.

> "Sustainability comes from synergy between the personal and professional parts of each employee's life."

Instead, we have created an environment in which the work itself also supports each employee's "life roadmap" and individual goals. Our teams work remotely and have a lot of autonomy, so they can design their workday to suit the demands of their lives. As long as the work gets done, where or when it gets done is not important. The act of working — solving complex problems, mastering new skills, and learning to lead — should make people better, not just at work but at life. Employees need to perform, but that does not mean they should not grow in the process. When employees get better, the business gets better.

As they master their work, it is also important to offer opportunities for career advancement. Appreciation is not just about praise. It is about the opportunity to rise based on your effort and accomplishments. Sustainably happy organizations promote from within and create a culture where every employee knows that achievement will be rewarded.

Some of those rewards should be financial. We are the only software company of our size I know of that offers profit sharing. We did it from the first day with our first employee. We want people to think of themselves as owners of the business and to think about the bottom line. When you have a stake in a business, you treat the company's money like it is your own. At a team dinner, you will think twice about having the $50 entree because it is coming out of your share of profits.

Profit sharing encourages a team to take ownership of everything that happens and focuses each team member on the success of customers and the company.

How Lovability Benefits Owners/Investors

For company owners and investors, it seems like lovability would have one benefit: profit. Profits are important, of course, but they are only one part of a bigger picture. Lovability yields other important benefits:

Stability

"Professional gamblers," the saying goes, "do not gamble." It means that amateurs might accept the house advantage but pros do everything they can to minimize risk. Owners and investors think the same way. They might accept risk as a necessary part of realizing a return but will still do everything they can to reduce their overall risk. Having a stake in a stable, well-run company with sustainable revenue growth can be just the thing to balance out a high-risk portfolio — especially for venture capitalists (which we discussed in chapter 2) who only hit a home run one out of every 10 times at bat, if they are lucky. When you consider the write-downs and other recent assaults on the value of promising but overhyped, could-be $1 billion startups, having a stable, boring, predictably profitable company looks pretty good.

Long-term financial payoff

Stable companies with happy workforces also perform better financially than high-anxiety, high-turnover businesses. Alex Edmans, professor of Finance at London Business School, showed that 28 years' worth of data reveals that companies with high employee satisfaction scores outperform their peer companies in long-run stock returns by 2.3 percent to 3.8 percent per year, even after controlling for other factors that drive returns.[5]

Answering the obvious chicken-and-egg question, Edmans concluded that it is happy employees who drive performance, not the other way around. That is proof that creating a company where employees feel great about what they do and why improves the bottom line.

Lower recruiting costs

The LinkedIn Talent Brand Index (TBI) rates how much prospective employees trust and want to work with a company. Internal LinkedIn research found that firms with the highest TBI reduced their hiring costs by as much as 50 percent, compared to their counterparts with low TBIs.[6]

But lovability does not just reduce recruitment costs. If you are known for a miserable, high-stress employee experience, you will pay well above market rate to attract even mediocre candidates to your company. You may not get top talent at any price. But if you have a lovable CPE, loyal customers, and a sustainably happy culture, you can hire the best without overpaying. You are also more likely to attract the kind of people who understand that a great job is not just about generous compensation but about growing and doing meaningful work.

A promising future

For the owner of a lovable company, the future looks better than today. You are working with purpose and building a product, team, and company that matters. Because you have built around sustainability and value, you are probably enjoying yourself and not looking around for your next venture. I cannot imagine anything else I could do that would be more rewarding than what I do every day.

Greater wealth

The value of a lovable company tends to increase over time. If you have developed one revenue stream that has earned customer love and loyalty, you can do it again . . . and again. That is predictable growth, and it is deeply reassuring to be able to predict significant growth in the future. Owners who prioritize lovability are more likely to be happy and still own their companies if and when a big payoff comes.

How Lovability Benefits Everyone

An emphasis on lovable products and companies also means less volatility in the economy in general. That is what I mean when I talk about a "lovability economy" — less volatility, fewer bubbles, and fewer sudden, disastrous declines like the collapse of the real estate market in 2007. With less tolerance for hype — and less speculative investment based on that hype — we will see more businesses earning their valuations based on great products and sound management. That would translate into fewer destructive failures costing tens if not hundreds of thousands of jobs. That is a real human cost that we would be much better off without.

Growth built on lovability is growth built on creating consistent value for customers and employees. It's growth based on substance — on giving people something meaningful, whether that is a job with purpose or a CPE that solves real problems and makes customers more productive. There are no shortcuts to lovable growth. You do not get there by way of snazzy presentations, raising tens of millions of dollars, and press releases, but through the humble, painstaking work of building relationships while putting people and values first.

Love breeds responsibility

It is hard to find many better examples of values-first leadership than Ventura, California-based outdoor clothing company Patagonia. For more than 30 years, the company has defied conventional wisdom by building its brand as much around environmental responsibility as on quality products and service. How many businesses would run a marketing campaign encouraging customers to not buy new products but repair the old ones instead in order to reduce their environmental footprint?

Only companies interested in creating a "lovability economy" would prioritize sustainable growth for themselves and the world and take a long-term perspective. They see themselves as stewards of meaningful relationships and understand that mutually positive interactions and exchanges of value are lasting.

Patagonia has even made its supply chain public with an online map showing every farm, textile mill, and factory it uses in sourcing its materials and manufacturing its products. Anyone who wants to can see where their Patagonia products come from and verify that the company is walking the walk — using sustainable materials and producing apparel in facilities that are safe for workers.

That is transparency that breeds trust. Founder Yvon Chouinard's vision has also led to a culture that is not only employee-friendly (the company even encourages employees at its corporate headquarters to quit early when the surf is up) but attracts people whose values align with the company's. This aggressively anti-profit, pro-values approach has yielded big dividends. The privately-held benefit corporation is tight-lipped about its revenues, but two years after it began its "cause marketing" campaign, sales increased 27 percent, to $575 million in 2013.[7]

But you do not have to pursue a cause marketing strategy to honor your responsibility to customers and realize sustainable growth. Being lovable brings deceptively simple requirements. Your customers want you to make good on your promises. You have a responsibility to them to follow through and ensure your commitments are delivered. But you also have a responsibility to yourself and your team.

Lovability means you are responsible for being your best. To achieve this, you must be accountable for setting the goals of the organization and sharing a clear plan of action. Each person needs to understand their unique value to the company and role in helping pursue its vision and goals. The more you honor that responsibility, the more the team will love you for it. Your job is to clear a path for growth by fighting back against destructive or invasive elements that would stand in your team's way.

Lovability is good business for everyone.

WORDS TO LOVE BY

- **Love is an essential, measurable business metric**
  It's too soft and squishy for some people, but nothing is more import-ant for assessing a company's sustainability or growth potential than the intensity of customer love. Tracking expressions of that love reveals how it changes over time and lets you pick out patterns that can reveal what you're doing right — and wrong.

- **Lovability benefits customers**
  It lets them know that your company shares their values, respects and cares about them, and will be around for the long haul. Lovable orga-nizations also produce cultures and people who are great at solving customers' problems and anticipating their needs — which, of course, leads to the virtuous cycle of more customer love.

- **Lovability benefits employees**
  It infuses their work with greater purpose and meaning. Instead of the myth of work-life balance, employees get a work experience that fits into their lives and helps them achieve more. It breeds a workplace cul-ture that helps employees be more engaged and lead more purposeful lives built on integrity. A lovable organization also rewards employees generously for their accomplishments with everything from career growth opportunities to profit sharing. The result is sustainable happi-ness, a culture that helps employees grow while attracting and retain-ing the best people and ensuring an exceptional Complete Product Experience.

- **Lovability benefits owners and investors**
  Growth is fueled in the short and long term while also reducing volatility. Because growth is based on substantive factors — values,

relationships, product quality, and excellent service — it's real, lasting, and replicable. Owners and investors who stay for the long haul can build new revenue streams around lovability and be on hand when growth turns into big financial reward.

♡ *Chapter Five*

CHASE VALUE, NOT VALUATION

If building lovable products and creating meaningful value over time makes so much sense, why do founders and product builders lose their way? That is an essential question in this book and one that you are probably wondering. But before I answer that, let's take a look at another company I know that is getting it right.

On June 1, 2016, *The New York Times* ran an article titled, "No Venture Capital Needed, or Wanted,"[1] about the lesser-known culture of startup founders who elect not to seek venture capital money and instead bootstrap their companies. The article featured Saatva, a mattress company that has grown to $120 million in revenues[2] since its founding in 2010. But it was not Saatva's growth that interested me. It was the comments on the company's website from its customers:

> *"I have had my mattress for a little over 60 days and I am in love. The purchase was very simple and easy to complete online with no hidden fees throughout the process. A few days after making my purchase I was sent an email containing details of my purchase and what to expect for delivery."*

"I emailed Saatva shortly after the delivery, told them it went splendidly, that the mattress was flawless, and that I had already slept on it and was in love with it. Only then did they take my credit card information — and that's when we quarreled over whether I would let them discount the mattress, etc. Let me put it this way: When's the last time you quarreled with a company over them being too generous with you?"

"WOW! I literally have never seen customer service like this from any company I have EVER dealt with. The responsiveness, the courtesy, the complete willingness to honor every element of their guarantee (. . . we swapped the mattress once, and then returned the second one . . . not necessarily obvious that their guarantee covered that). This is a memorable company . . ."

"This was the best decision ever. I received it sooner than expected and we love it. No more aches and pains when we get up in the morning. According to a tracking device I recently received, I was getting an average of 3 – 4 hours of sleep every night. Now with the new Saatva, I am getting 6 – 7 hours of sleep per night. I would recommend anyone who has any doubt to just try it out. I promise you'll love it."

Nearly every customer review is that enthusiastic, but what also stands out is that customers are praising not just the company's product, but the Complete Product Experience (CPE), from sales to the delivery personnel who came to their homes to set up their new sleep systems.

Love Sets You Free

Saatva has grown from an initial $350,000 investment by co-founder Ron Rudzin to an expected $180 million in revenue in 2016, largely because of lovability. It is an example of lovability's greatest benefit to entrepreneurs — the power to free them from needing to spend precious time looking for investors to fund their businesses. Building an organization whose priority is to deliver an experience that transcends customer expectations is more than good business. It lets you build your way, according to your values.

Let's consider another similar story — the dating website Plenty of Fish. German programmer Markus Frind started the company in 2003 as a programming exercise. He had been wanting to learn a new coding language called *ASP.NET*, so he built the site in two weeks — and to his surprise, it took off. Frind never raised a dime of outside money, because the venture was profitable from the beginning. "I didn't see the need to raise money because I wouldn't know what to do with it," he said in a 2015 interview with *Business Insider*. "It was a profitable company, and there was no need to raise money."[3]

Plenty of Fish grew slowly and organically for more than 10 years, eventually growing to about 75 employees and 90 million registered users. In 2015, Match Group (which also owns dating sites Match.com and OKCupid) bought Plenty of Fish for $575 million. "It wasn't like I had a plan to create a dating site," Frind said. "It was just a side project I created that got really big." Not bad for what started as a hobby.

Saatva and Plenty of Fish are examples of what is possible, even if they are uncommon today. At the other extreme is mobile payments startup Clinkle. In 2013, the company received a record (at the time) $25 million in seed funding from major Silicon Valley players like Peter Thiel, Andreessen Horowitz, and Marc Benioff, despite not having a publicly available product. However, Clinkle could not get a working version of its wireless mobile wallet technology to market. By 2015, founder and CEO Lucas Duplan was trying to engineer a sale to Apple or Google even as employees were quitting in protest. Finally, a January 2016 story in *Forbes* indicated that some early Clinkle investors were asking for their money back.[4] Today, the Clinkle website simply consists of a blank page bearing this sentence: "If you would like access to your account history, please email support@treatsapp.com." As this book goes to press, the future of Clinkle looks bleak.

Groupon: A Cautionary Tale

Despite the repeated flameouts of companies like Clinkle, conventional thinking in the business world remains mostly unchanged: Pursue the highest possible valuation for your business in the shortest possible time. That conventional wisdom makes it hard to do the one thing that makes success far more likely — build lovable products that create value for people.

Valuation is certainly more glamorous than value. Valuation is the value of an asset, usually calculated by an expert. For an early stage company that is seeking outside funding, its valuation is basically set by investors who want to invest a certain amount of money and own a certain percentage of the company. That means it is highly qualitative based on a number of variables including: investor interest, the perceived market opportunities, the experience of the team, and the current investing. Value, on the other hand, is a measure of the importance, usefulness, or worth of something. Compared to valuation, where words like billions are thrown around, value is dull. However, if your goal is to build something lovable, it is anything but.

Groupon is a study of the hazards of pursuing scale and valuation at all costs. In 2010, *Forbes* called it the "fastest growing company ever" after its founders raised $135 million in funding, giving Groupon a valuation of more than $1 billion after just 17 months.[5] The company turned down a $6 billion acquisition offer from Google and went public in 2011 with one of the biggest IPOs since Google's in 2004.[6] It was one of the original unicorns.

However, the business model had serious problems. Groupon sometimes sold so many Daily Deals that participating businesses were overwhelmed . . . even crippled. Other businesses accused Groupon of strong-arming them to sign up for Daily Deals. Customers started to view the group discount (the company's bread and butter) as a sign that a participating business was desperate. Businesses stopped signing up. Journalists suggested that Groupon was prioritizing customer acquisition over retention — growth over value — and that it had gone public before it had a solid, proven business model.[7]

Groupon is still a player, with just over $3 billion in annual revenue in 2015. But its stock has fallen from $26 a share to about $4 today, and it has withdrawn from many international markets. Also revealing is that the company is suing IBM for patent infringement, something that will not create customer value.[8]

Many promising startups have paid the price for rushing to scale. We can see clues to potential future failures in the recent "down rounds" (stock purchases priced at a lower valuation than those of previous investors) hitting companies like Foursquare, Gilt Group, Jet, Jawbone, and Technorati. In their rush to build scale, executives and founders search for shortcuts to sustainable, long-term revenue growth.

The Venture Trap

The best business are usually tortoises, not hares — slow and steady, relying on personal relationships and responsiveness to grow sales, create value, and build customer trust. When payment infrastructure company Stripe was in a private beta back in 2011, co-founders Patrick and John Collison paid special attention to early adopters from the Y Combinator alumni network, going to their offices personally and facilitating developer meet ups. Stripe now has a ferociously loyal customer and developer base and was valued at $5 billion after an investment from Visa in 2015.[9]

The troubling trend is not the companies with flawed business models or poor products. It is the ones with solid strategies and plenty of customers who go to market and then spend much of their time and resources creating buzz, raising money, and building their valuation. Many have quality products and are run by smart people; they could thrive for decades. Instead, they chase lottery-winning dreams instead of working on the fundamentals. In the process, they turn away from the only thing that matters — creating customer value by delivering a lovable CPE.

That is the "venture trap." Company founders, caught in the cycle of spin and breathless rumor about high valuations, place growth above all other goals. The desire to build a big business fast, amass vast personal wealth, and be one of the movers and shakers written up in *The Wall Street Journal* and *VentureBeat* motivates some founders to throw caution to the wind in favor of hype and misleading behavior. The cost can be insurmountable.

There is nothing wrong with thinking big, aspiring to scale, and wanting to build a billion-dollar business. And as I suggested in chapter 2, certain types of businesses require costly, long-term investments to build out their CPE. But too often entrepreneurs and product builders go wrong and steer onto the rocks when they focus on raising and then quickly making money before they build something that people love. Money is both a tool and an outcome, not a product. Create something that people love and success will follow. Without that, hype and financial wizardry can only add up to disaster.

Every few years, a wave of "the rules have changed" thinking becomes popular in Silicon Valley and other global innovation epicenters. It follows a predictable cycle. First, the economy gains steam and venture investors and entrepreneurs quickly decide that the fundamentals of building a meaningful business have changed. We saw this in the dot-com collapse and recently in the Great Recession caused by the belief that the rules of mortgage lending had ceased to exist.

"Money is both a tool and an outcome, not a product. Create something that people love and success will follow."

Next, flush with cash and the certainty that they're reinventing how business is done, the most adventurous among us launch companies. Some are built on visionary ideas. Most are not. Many of these ventures fail and for a while people return to proven models of building businesses: value, sales, and profits. But memories fade.

Next, a new crop of company builders comes to town and the hype machine revs up all over again. However, the outcome never changes. For every truly transformative idea that mints new billionaires, there are a thousand failures. It is not a question of whether or not the hype machine will be running — it will. It is a question of whether you will climb on it or choose a more conservative, sustainable path.

Rushing to the Exits

If some company founders are guilty of chasing hype-inflated valuation over real growth, others are guilty of bolting when times get tough. Upfront Ventures partner Mark Suster writes about this on his blog, *Both Sides of the Table*. In a post titled "Is Going for Rapid Growth Always Good? Aren't Startups So Much More?" he pointed out that the industry is often too quick to believe that things are "up and to the right" — and just as quick to move onto the next big thing. But he also noted that entrepreneurs fall into the same line of thinking when they jump to pivot or sell in an "acquihire."

Suster said that you can follow the mania for instant growth up the value chain. "[Limited Partners] LPs (the people who invest in VC funds) want to know what 'hot' deals you're in. 'What exits have you had?' What, since '09? If I exited those wouldn't it sort of been a . . . failure? I'm shooting for 7-to-10-year exits. Most LPs are not. They want to know that you're in Twitter, Facebook, Square, Fab and the like."[10]

Exit-fast thinking is anti-customer. Loyal customers are the reason a business has value in the first place. An entrepreneur who makes their exit strategy their priority is sabotaging their own business without realizing it.

Investors often throw so much cash at startups that founders become instant millionaires, leaving them with less motivation to build something extraordinary. Whereas venture capitalists used to invest in startups so that founders could use those funds to build the business, today the order can be somewhat scrambled. Instead of gaining wealth and accolades once their business succeeds, some startup founders pocket some of the money they raise — without ever having to build a meaningful and lasting business.

> "Exit-fast thinking is anti-customer.
> Loyal customers are the reason a business
> has value in the first place."

"Build to exit" encourages shortcuts. Instead, build something that you feel good about and love working in. You will create products that earn customer love, grow organically and authentically, and build a valuation based on solid fundamentals, not promises. The key to a prosperous exit is not to think about the exit at all. Simply do exceptional things for people over and over again. Then when a buyer makes you an offer, you might be shocked at the real enterprise value you have created.

Paul Zuber, a friend and operating partner at Thoma Bravo with a platinum record of technology startups and acquisitions, shared this story: "Andy Grove was asked what his exit strategy was when he started Intel. He laughed and said there was no exit strategy. That's what attracted me when I worked at Sun. That's what's important: that sense of mission and working for a bigger purpose. That should be embodied in a product and a company."

Beautiful Distractions

So, what is really going on here? Why are so many of us irresistibly attracted to big dollars that come with all types of gotchas and shiny concepts that provide no real value? I get asked about this all the time and I have identified five distractions that preoccupy the attention of most startup teams. Avoid these at all costs.

1. Raising lots of money

You are probably getting the point by now. I think you should fund your business and avoid taking other people's money for as long as you possibly can. And if you do not think that is very long, maybe you should wait a bit longer before starting your own company.

I was talking with a former colleague who received funding for his company, and he told me excitedly that he expected to be retired and living in a villa in Tuscany in five years . . . even though his company doesn't have a product or any customers. That's not only putting the wine before the grapes but the land, too.

We all crave financial independence. It is a very human desire to have complete control over our lives. Entrepreneurs see billion-dollar company valuations, amplified by media hype, and fantasize about their own fortunes.

But common sense has to kick in at some point. Without it, the quest for money will overshadow the goal of building a viable business.

In late 2014, Mixpanel co-founder Suhail Doshi claimed that his company would soon be valued at more than $1 billion. After a $65 million investment from Andreessen Horowitz valued the business at $865 million, that prediction looked like a good one. But in April 2016, Doshi admitted that after spending big to fuel growth, Mixpanel was changing its focus to cost-cutting. Showing admirable self-awareness, he admitted in interviews with reporters that the company's previous strategy was growth for growth's sake, with ego getting in the way.[11]

Disrupted, Dan Lyons's best-selling book about the year he spent working at HubSpot, tells a similar story. Lyons makes the point that while technology companies that show real longevity grow around a revolutionary product or technology, startups like HubSpot often spend heavily before they have a product that customers want. Burdened with heavy expenses, they must then pursue revenue at any cost to show growth and raise more capital. HubSpot went public in 2014 and had an $880 million valuation, but it still operates at a loss. In February 2016, the Associated Press reported that HubSpot shares had fallen 48 percent since the beginning of the year.[12] The only goal seems to be "getting big fast."

The irony is that the odds of building a startup into a company worth more than $1 million are vanishingly small. According to *First Round Review*, the chance of building a billion-dollar company is .00006 percent.[13] Those are the same odds as your vote being the one vote that decides a presidential election.[14]

2. Building a Minimum Viable Product (MVP)

When an organization's priority becomes growth at all costs, it pulls people and resources away from developing products and delivering a great CPE. I can confirm from personal experience that it takes everything you have to serve your early customers so well that they help you acquire new customers and grow your company.

The growth-first gospel sometimes leads startups to release what the Lean

Startup school of thought calls the Minimum Viable Product (MVP). This is the most basic version of a product, with just enough features to be usable. The thinking is that the product leader and their team will circle back to the MVP at some point and fully develop it into a great product. But that rarely happens.

In a marketplace where customers have few alternatives, the MVP philosophy can fuel growth. But today's consumer has many products to choose from in virtually any category — especially in technology. In this world, the MVP strategy is a deathtrap. It aims for "good enough," not great. It produces products that sort of work but never delight. It breeds an employee culture that is about making the sale, not making the customer fall in love.

John Peters, CEO and veteran of many Silicon Valley startup turn-arounds, told me about a similar problem in venture capital. Investors obsess over "actionable intellectual capital" that can be patented and licensed, he said. This compels startups to throw concerns about building a meaningful product over the side of the boat in order to create technology that can be patented.

In a choice-rich world, the customer's relationship with technology is transactional. Basic features and protected intellectual property are nice but the key to growth is differentiation through long-term customer happiness. That comes when customers adore your product or service and want you to succeed.

3. Hiring a sales team

Chris and I always wanted to build an organization that did not insert sales-people between the product creators and the customer. We wanted to create something where salespeople were unnecessary because the product — and the experience the customer had using it — were so satisfying that people bought instead of being sold to. We aspired to eliminate friction and put employees in a position to put the customer's interests first.

Traditional sales puts salespeople in the compromised position of trying to appear like they have the *customer's* interests at heart when they really have *their own* wallet in mind. Commission-based sales structures create a moral dilemma that customers are wise to. They view selling as coercive and adversarial. Think Alec Baldwin in *Glengarry Glen Ross*.

I never liked that character and I definitely never wanted to be him. That is why I will never hire a salesperson. I prefer an approach I call "Never Be Closing." If your mission is to create lovability and provide an exceptional CPE, forget everything you know about sales. Customers have access to vast amounts of product information. They just need someone to help them find solutions and figure out what is best for them — even if it's not your product. If your product is not good, no salesperson will make it lovable.

At Aha! we have replaced sales with Customer Success. Our Customer Success team solves problems and anticipates customer needs before customers know they have them. We do not hire traditional sales or support people. We hire only former product managers to work with our customers, and nobody earns a commission. Instead of selling, Customer Success helps our customers get the most out of the time they spend using our software.

I travel a lot and at the Alhambra in Granada, Spain, I realized that the best Customer Success people are like great tour guides. They understand that their fundamental job is to share what they know and to ensure that their customers have a meaningful experience.

Both share many qualities:

- They are knowledgeable, sometimes spending years studying their domain, and have gained deep insights.

- They are empathetic and understand that it is not always easy to immerse yourself in something new.

- They are genuine, eager to share what they know because their knowledge and experience excites them.

- They are relaxed. They have no hidden agendas and are confident in presenting diverse perspectives.

- They are dependable. They show up on time and are responsive to questions because they know curiosity is a teacher's best friend.

But the biggest reason we have turned away from traditional sales has to do with motivation. All great guides are motivated by intrinsic rewards. It's not a profession to pursue to get rich. They want to lead because it is in their nature to help and share what they know. Their passion fuels their work. And their professional success ultimately depends on their client's success and their joy of learning. That leads to love, enthusiastic referrals, steady growth . . . and no need for strong-armed sales.

> "If your product is not good, no salesperson
> will make it lovable."

4. Renting expensive office space

It is considered common knowledge that you need a headquarters to build a company. Everyone does it because it seems like a sound investment — get people in the same location, build camaraderie, have a place to bring customers and backers, and so on. A 2014 Priceonomics survey of 54 Y Combinator companies found that the median company spent $6,100 a month on rent, which does not seem like much.[15]

But when you are trying to build a great product and a sustainable base of loyal customers with no outside investment, every dollar counts. And $73,000 a year actually matters. Also, concentrating your team in an office means your hiring pool is mostly limited to people in your geographic region. That is why Aha! has never had a central office. Talented, dedicated people are everywhere, and most are happier staying where they are. The Internet and videoconferencing technology make our recruitment pool global and our facility costs zero. How good does that sound?

Distributed teams make it possible to hire the best people wherever they are, avoid expensive talent bidding wars, and avoid catching the lease madness of technology hotbeds like San Francisco, Los Angeles, New York, London, and Melbourne. That is one reason that remote work among the non-self-employed has grown 103 percent since 2005.[16]

Your business may need a central office someday, but hold off for as long as possible. You can still be professional while operating out of your home office and many of your customers probably support remote work as well. You will save on rent and secondary overhead costs, including utilities, furnishings, insurance, and signage. Most importantly, your team will be able to work where they work best.

5. Eating steak and lobster

It is great to be optimistic about the future as long as you temper that optimism with a dose of reality and some common sense. That is not what we saw back in the dot-com boom of the late 1990s, when the lavish spending of venture-backed companies — renting entire hotel floors for parties, buying commercial time during the Super Bowl — led to a ruinous cash burn rate and so many company implosions.

The same thing appears to be happening again. I keep hearing troubling stories about startups sending employees to speak at far-away conferences, building fancy new offices, and regularly splurging on expensive meals and entertainment. Founders with pockets full of investor cash are offering huge salary packages, running expensive marketing and PR campaigns, designing "adult playroom" offices, and wooing talent with some extreme perks — including, according to one recruiter, an in-house mixed martial arts octagon.

A little spending spree is fine when you have plenty of cash in the bank. But, as I have discussed, investor money is not free. It often comes with expectations of unnatural growth and a big exit. Extravagance pulls your focus from the only thing that matters — creating extraordinary products and experiences that delight customers and win their loyalty.

Reckless spending also becomes a habit. Do you really need that "ball pit" in the office for employees to sit in when they are feeling stressed out or to buy thousands of orange and black balloons for Halloween or to rent out the local football stadium for your holiday party? Waste should *never* be normal. Survival means being a realist and saying "No." Disregard everything that is not tied to creating an exceptional CPE. Your other goals will still be there when you are profitable.

> "Extravagance pulls your focus away from the only thing that matters — creating extraordinary products and experiences that delight customers and win their loyalty."

Too many emerging companies and experienced entrepreneurs find themselves mesmerized by these shiny objects. But remember, they are distractions from your business, not your business itself. Investing in any of them is a mistake that can leave even those with the best intentions broke and wondering, "What happened?"

Both of These Things Should Be More Like the Other

Now, there is one group of businesses that could stand to show more risky, innovative behavior: large, established "legacy" companies. Decades-old corporations tend to be conservative about growth — refining their products, building relationships, and finding early adopters who are invested in the long-term success of the business. They look for ways to reduce risk and increase their odds of building what customers love.

Consider taking that approach with your startup. It requires confidence, boldness, sacrifice, and perseverance, because you will be bucking the "grow first, grow fast" ethos. We could never have taken that approach at Aha! if we had not believed that it gave us the best chance for success. We were fortunate to have the experience and confidence to be different. We are humbled to have been given the chance to prove that doing what we *thought* was right actually was.

Ironically, while startups often take too many risks, established companies rarely take enough. Fear drives their decision making because they have more to lose. They stumble over the idea of the MVP in a different way from startups. While a new company might be too quick to roll out something riddled with bugs, a legacy company might have a solid product that they cannot get to market because they fret over every detail. If you will not release a product until it is "perfect," you will never release it at all.

Instead of hiring a new sales team for a new product, a large company might siphon off a small tiger team from an existing sales team and incentivize them to sell the new product. But they will also expect them to hit the sales targets for their established products. The new product never gets mind share or sales priority and is guaranteed to fail or be de-funded because it cannot compete with the existing, established products on revenue.

If you are running an established company, try behaving like a reckless startup once in a while. Explore new opportunities, take bold action based on some new insights, leverage emerging technologies, and go all-in on an exciting project with no distractions. Be willing to remove your best and brightest people from day-to-day distractions so they can create the innovations that will be the future of your organization.

Time for the Minimum Lovable Product (MLP)

There is not much data on technology product failures. However, research by Shikhar Ghosh of Harvard Business School shows that about 75 percent of venture-backed firms in the U.S. fail to return investors' capital.[17] That is failure, and with that comes a lot of failed products. Like *The Hunger Games*, the odds are not in your favor. So why play the usual game?

As I discussed earlier in this chapter, the MVP mindset is fool's gold. In our increasingly transactional world, real growth comes from long-term customer happiness. That occurs when customers love your product or service and not only want to do business with you but want your company to thrive. Whether you are running an emerging company or one that has been around for a century, it's time for a new approach to product development.

Your products should grow customer love, not be an obstacle to it. Set aside the distractions of scale and valuation and build something new. I call it the Minimum Lovable Product (MLP). Instead of launching with basic functionality and a promise to add more in the future, MLPs solve problems and delight customers right out of the box. Their goal is not to make customers say, "Well, it works," but to exclaim, "This is brilliant!"

The MLP approach is messy. Most engineers avoid "squishy" matters like learning what makes customers smile or feel relief. That's okay — that is why engineers and product managers must collaborate to make MLPs. While engineers move the ones and zeroes, product managers move hearts and minds and act as the voice of the customer.

A focus on love will change how you do business, because business becomes about creating value. You have to get out in the world and find out what constitutes value in the minds of your customers. The goal is no longer creating what people think is cool but creating what the customer cannot live without. Never guess at what your customers value, because it may not be what you think it is or what investors tell you. Get your hands dirty, talk to them, find out, build it, and use it yourself.

Minimum Viable Product (MVP) Principles	VS	Minimum Lovable Product (MLP) Principles
Goal is to increment		Goal is to disrupt
Problem cannot be understood		Problem can be understood
Market cannot be analyzed		Market can be analyzed
Customers do not know what they want		Customers know what they want
Few product alternatives exist		Many product alternatives exist
Avoid architecture decisions because technology is unpredictable		Make architecture decisions because technology is sufficiently stable
Lean effort because success is unlikely		Dedicated effort to the opportunity
Pivot		Focus
Customers tolerate your product		Customers love your product

Lovability is not new. It is the way our grandparents and great-grandparents did business. It is the way many old-guard companies were built. Customer delight and the MLP have always worked, but they have gotten lost in the glare and glamour of big money, big egos, and confused teams.

> "Never guess at what your customers value, because it may not be what you think it is or what investors tell you."

Keep it simple. Put your head down, ignore the hype, and focus on your customers. Learn what they care about, what they need, and what makes their lives better. Then build that. Eliminate distractions and drama that keep your team from doing their finest work. Do everything you can to deliver value that your customers will not only recognize but sacrifice for. You will get emails like this gem sent to Aha! from a customer on the verge of convincing his company to use our software company-wide:

> *"I am now in the final stages of our internal procurement process and the purchase requisition is being processed tomorrow . . . I will forgo any onboarding or possibly a kidney for the luxury of one more week using the Aha! trial!!"*

The Watney Rule

Consultant and SalesLogix co-founder Greg Head summed it up well when he wrote in a blog post, "Most startups shouldn't expect to raise equity capital funding."[18] Most do not, and that is a good thing. Venture funding *increases* your odds of failure by taking your eye off the ball.

Sure, if you build a product with venture funding in mind, investors might fund your startup. You might be written up in *Fast Company*. But that is not a predictor that customers will delight in what you give them — and that is the strongest predictor of success. Create intense lovability and, like Aha!, you might not need venture funding at all.

I am a fan of what some call the "Watney Rule," named for the fictional character Mark Watney in the film *The Martian*. Stranded on Mars, Watney is forced to find a way to grow potatoes to sustain his life in case a rescue ship cannot reach him for years. For companies, the rule means, "Be self-sustaining so you do not need help."

Because we did not seek investors for Aha! or take any outside investment, we answer only to our customers and each other. We grow our own way, at our own pace, and put the customer at the center of everything. We track our progress against organic, simple goals like "Make sure Aha! is a joy to use" and "Deliver on the Aha! promise." How do we measure if we are successful? Eighty percent of new product features are the direct result of what customers ask us for. That is our success metric.

Every business — from startups to intrapreneurial groups within established companies — needs space to think big and put customer value first. That does not fit the "scale at all costs" model, but it works if your goal is to build something that lasts. Lovability is easier to create when you only answer to the people who you need to love you for a very long time.

WORDS TO LOVE BY

- **Lovability frees you from outside investment**
  Customer love fuels organic, sustainable growth and removes the pressure to seek investors and stoke hype to inflate your company's value.

- **You cannot build something great by only looking at the exits**
  There's nothing wrong with wanting to generate wealth over time from the business you build. But a quick-exit strategy makes the business all about you and future promises, and not the customer, or your team. This actually makes it harder to do right and do well.

- **Entrepreneurs are often distracted by five shiny concepts**
  These are the five concepts that blind too many of us from a better way: Making raising money the top priority; rushing to market with a Minimum Viable Product (MVP); hiring a sales team; leasing a big office; and wasting money on reckless expenditures.

- **It is time for the Minimum Lovable Product (MLP)**
  Your customers should exclaim, "That's awesome!" when they use your product and interact with your team — not mutter, "That's OK." This means you need to throw everything away that you have learned about going lean and creating an MVP. It's time to focus all of your energy on building an MLP.

- **Startups and established businesses should learn from each other**
  Startups should show more of the conservatism of established companies and grow steadily while focusing on customer value. Established companies should exhibit some of the risk-taking chutzpah of startups.

- **The Watney Rule**

  Grow your own food in case help never comes. Rather than chase outside funding, make your business sustainable and profitable as quickly as you can so you never need outside help. Control your own future and prosper.

Part III

CREATING LOVABILITY

Chapter Six

THE OLD WAYS ARE NEW AGAIN

Creating product lovability is not just a matter of wishing it to be so and establishing a set of policies and procedures that demand it. It is not even about hiring the right people, though you cannot create lovability without the right people who buy fully into your vision. Everything begins with the philosophy behind your business — the reason you are in business. That is your real story. It's called purpose.

When Chris Waters and I were starting Aha!, we kept coming back to the same question: "What problem do we want to help customers solve and how can we solve it better than anyone else?" That question forms the heart of an organization's strategy and defines its mission. We knew that it could not be about us or our past success. It was about solving the right problem in a unique way and hiring the right people who had the same passion to serve our customers.

Challenge number one was identifying the customer problem that we wanted to solve. That came quickly: Help product managers set better strategy and create visual roadmaps. We wanted to help companies build better products. We wanted product teams to be happy doing it. When we launched, customers immediately told us that our software was what they had been desperately looking for. We thought we had succeeded, but that was not why they loved us.

What set us apart from the beginning was how we helped our customers solve problems and how we made them feel. When they needed us we stopped in our tracks to help. We put them first and everything else second. We still do the same thing today. Isn't that what we all want? I hate waiting and feeling like I am not a priority. I'll bet you do, too. When I call a company and hear a recorded message say, "Your call is very important to us," I cannot help thinking, "If it was so important, you would have a live person answering it."

When I have a problem or need, I want someone to help me. I do not want to wait hours or until the next day. That "urgency degradation" tells me that your company is excited about having me as a customer . . . until you close the sale. After that, I am an annoyance.

We have intentionally gone in the other direction. Aha! has a long-term, people-centric philosophy. We take care of the customer who needs us right now, period. Nothing else matters. It is the only way we know to build a meaningful, sustainable company. We thought that was obvious, so we were surprised to learn that it set us apart.

But we have not always been as committed to being ultra-responsive. We built our previous companies with a people-centric, responsive approach as well, because that is just part of our DNA. But being completely interrupt-driven and responsive to customer needs did not define those businesses.

Were they successful? Yes. Would we have built them the same way knowing what we know now? No. Why not? Because we were distracted, and that kept us from being solely focused on the happiness of the customer.

We spent lots of time presenting to potential investors, raising money, and meeting with our board of directors. That was what we knew and saw all around us in Silicon Valley. Did that pull some of our focus away from building a lovable product? Sure. Did it make us less able to respond to customers instantly, the way we like to be responded to? Absolutely.

We still built meaningful products that created value. Later those products were acquired and are still delivering customer value today. But because of those experiences, we learned to stay true to what we believe and found that there is an even better way to run a company.

Now we want to share what we got right and help you avoid our mistakes.

Old-Fashioned Values

Our past companies did well, but we knew we could do better. We wanted to build something that we felt good about, that did things the right way, and made people's lives better while being profitable. To do that, we knew we needed to start not with technology and products but *values*.

Aha! is that business. We have built it around a set of core values that have become part of the company's lineage — values that are "grandpa-inspired." They're old-fashioned ideas inspired by how our grandparents and the business owners of their time ran their businesses. They weren't running software companies, of course. They were operating corner grocery stores, optometry clinics, and restaurants. Their customers weren't across the world or contacting them through email. They were their neighbors. To make their businesses grow, our grandparents had to put integrity first and care about serving other people.

To us, it is silly to say, "It's not personal, it's just business." Business has always been personal. Unfortunately, that idea is the first casualty of the valuation-over-value model. In building Aha!, we wanted to take a different approach — not only from how we built our previous companies, but from the predominant way Silicon Valley companies are built. We wanted to steer clear of the predominant thinking with its flameouts and human collateral damage.

That kind of thinking tends to hurt employees the most. I discussed the challenges that result from focusing on valuation in the previous chapter. It is a major distraction and sometimes can be even worse. Let me share what can happen when some growth is combined with hyper-inflated expectations.

Investor favorite (and *Forbes* 2014 Hottest Startup) Zenefits, which sells companies employee health insurance plans and free software to manage those plans, was hit by scandal when it came out that many of its employees were not licensed to sell insurance. Not only did the company let 17 percent of its workforce go,[1] it repriced its stock at a much lower valuation, an action that may have cost ex-employees who exercised their stock options based on the higher valuation of millions of dollars. Worst of all, there has been talk that some current and former employees could face criminal charges.[2] It's bad to lose your job. It's worse to go to jail for doing your job.

Customers suffer, too. In 2014, 4chan founder Chris Poole announced that his artist community/drawing app startup Canvas would shut down. Not because it was not getting traction; the six-employee company had 1.4 million downloads of its DrawQuest app, more than half a million registered users, and 25,000 daily users who had collectively made 8 million drawings. But Canvas was not growing fast enough to allow it to return investors' capital and Poole saw no strategy that would make that happen. With nobody willing to buy it, the company would intentionally wind down to full stop.[3]

> "Business has always been personal."

As failures go, this was relatively gentle. Poole and his team informed customers and kept their application and servers running long enough so they could download their favorite drawings. Then it evaporated, leaving customers without support or the product they enjoyed. Think about how crazy that would sound to our grandparents — a young company with hundreds of thousands of enthusiastic customers, making money, forced to shut down and abandon those customers because it was not growing fast enough. That is the harm the current mindset around company building can inflict on everyone involved in the business.

There is another way.

An American Success Story

We are always looking for inspiration at Aha!, and typically that means finding a cutting-edge approach. But this time we looked to our past, to how our parents, grandparents, and even great-grandparents worked, built their businesses, and served their customers. What made them successful? We wanted to rediscover the unhindered effort, personal care, and relationship building that is mostly absent these days.

We looked at Chris's father, who was a chemist (what we call a pharmacist in the U.S.) in New Zealand. If customers were too old or sick to come to his store, he would personally drive prescriptions to their homes. It was not part of his "business model." It was the decent thing to do. His first job was to take care of people.

My maternal great-grandfather, Isidore Manpearl, left Poland in the early 1900s and traveled to New York looking for a brighter future. He walked the streets seeking work — any work. His tenacity paid off when a clothing manufacturer hired him as a seamster. He worked hard and over time became a shift supervisor and then a facility manager. Then he saw an opportunity to build something lasting.

Many historians consider the 1920s to be the decade that fashion entered the modern era. Manufacturing innovations made it easy to produce affordable clothing. It was also when hats became popular. Women began to wear more comfortable and stylish clothes and cut their hair short (a radical move at first) to fit under stylish new hats to further showcase their personality. All classes of men wore hats as well, even boys selling newspapers on the street corners.

Grandpa Isidore was at the center of this fashion transformation. He built multiple hat factories to meet the surging demand. From the 1930s to the 1950s, New York was the world's leading millinery city. A workforce of immigrants just like him, bolstered by relentless ambition, helped business in the Garment District boom.

He retired at 50 years old after selling his hat empire so he could move West to invest in real estate and pursue his passion for writing, and he lived to be 96. It's a classic American success story. But it would not have been possible if my great-grandfather had not focused on hard work or had been distracted from building exactly what customers wanted. Every hat he sold was a sign that he was selling value. That is a reminder that real product value precedes any meaningful company valuation.

Meaningful Human Interactions

The people who founded companies in past generations did not rely on massive funding and market hype to launch their businesses. Instead, they saw a genuine customer need — say, for well-made hats at a reasonable price in Brooklyn and the Bronx — and started a business to satisfy it. While many failed simply because running a business has always been challenging, most bent over backwards to make sure customers were satisfied. On this foundation they built household names like A&P and JCPenney.

The entrepreneurs of that era found intrinsic value in providing a meaningful product that improved their customers' lives while making a living that improved their own future. They generally did not think in terms of "How much will I be worth?" Instead, they focused on operating efficiently so they could keep the doors open, providing value for people, and building something that would prosper after they passed it on to their children. They thought about their legacy, and that meant more than cash.

Because technology in 1900 was limited to about 600,000 telephone users connected by switchboard operators, business was based on human interactions. That forced us to care about people. Relationships were the coin of the realm. Take a look at an old black and white photo of Flatbush Avenue in Brooklyn or any other commercial street from the first half of the twentieth century and you will see that most of the businesses are named after their proprietors. Your name was on the wall. People associated you with the quality of the product you delivered. I have a great old picture of the de Haaffs, my ancestors, who were fishmongers in Rotterdam, Holland. They are standing in front of a warehouse near their large truck, with the name *de Haaff* carved in granite above them.

Not that long ago, the hype machine did not exist. You called customers on a rotary phone. Word of mouth was your growth engine and it worked one person at a time. The only way you got people to recommend your business was to deliver value, provide great service, and get to know and care about your customers.

Investment instruments existed, but they were limited and largely off limits to small business owners. If you needed financing, you took out a personal loan from a family member or your neighborhood bank if you had one. Your business had to earn a profit to survive — there were no "freemium" models backed by wads of venture cash. You had to align the price you charged with the value you delivered and you had to get paid, because you had real costs and no way to operate in the red. If you could not turn a profit, you went under.

Twin Curses

Most small business owners still build on personal interaction and relationships. Many technology companies do not, often for good reason. It is expensive to hire a team of engineers to address challenges that have not been solved before. And, as I have pointed out, for some types of companies, it is impossible to build a meaningful product without a lot of initial cash and follow-on funding. Think about the resources required to build a network service, a new hardware platform for storing data, or a drug discovery business.

However, the last 10 years have brought exciting changes. The democratization of data center infrastructure means you can rent it inexpensively. The global reach of the Internet means you can make your service available to anyone. Low-cost, high-powered computing devices mean almost anyone is a potential customer. For many technology companies, massive funding is no longer mandatory.

But if that is the case, why did more than half of the nearly $60 billion invested by venture capitalists in 2015[4] go to seed and early stage companies? Why do software companies, which have so many resources that let them approach building their companies as small business owners of the past did, continue to receive the highest level of funding?

There are many explanations, but two primary reasons — curses — have led founders away from connection and responsiveness:

1. **Greed**

   It took Sears, Roebuck and Co. 52 years to approach $1 billion in sales. Jet.com, an Amazon rival, reached a $1 billion valuation in just four months in 2015.[5] Take an abundance of venture capital looking to be put to work, add investors eagerly seeking the next Facebook, and stir with hype and you get a potential wealth machine that blinds everyone involved.

2. Technology

It is a benefit and a curse. Technology has given us the ability to communicate with people at scale quickly and cost-effectively. But we have convinced ourselves that those costly, pesky human interactions and relationships are not really necessary anymore and engineered them out of the process. When we become all about valuation and growth, human interactions stop being the reason we are in business. We delude ourselves into believing we can distance ourselves from customers and still provide a high-value Complete Product Experience (CPE).

For decades, checking out at the supermarket was a personal experience. If you were a repeat customer, you got to know certain cashiers. You would ask about their day and they would ask about your kids. You felt connected to the store. But a few years ago, markets introduced self-serve checkout lanes, supposedly for convenience. Let's be honest: The change was less about customer convenience and more about cutting cashier salaries.

Self-serve lines are actually slower, aren't they? Sometimes, you just want someone to help you. For the sake of saving a few dollars, some businesses have robbed themselves of the personal touch that made them unique.

"Not that long ago, the hype machine did not exist. The only way you got people to recommend your business was to deliver value, provide great service, and get to know and care about your customers."

Shalleen Mayes, who works on the marketing team at Aha!, said the same about her banking. "My bank, Chase, took out the drive-through lanes to force customers to use their ATM to make deposits. Part of the reason I liked to bank there was the human connection with the tellers. This may be an effort to be more efficient, but it makes me love them a whole lot less. I complained."

Interestingly, she was not the only customer to complain about the change. Chase Bank actually listened and eventually brought back the drive-through lanes — rebuilding some of the lost love in the process.

Be Efficient and Human

There's the key word: love. Customers do not fall in love with automated systems. They resent what phone trees and automated support chat bots imply — that companies see their customers as an impediment to business. Even worse, it implies that companies think their customers are too unsophisticated to realize that it is about avoiding one-to-one interactions. You may not think that, but that is the message such policies and systems send.

You can automate your interactions (which is mandatory if you want your business to scale) and be efficient while keeping a human face. Give customers the information they need to self-serve but be incredibly responsive when they need to interact with you. Customers fall in love with companies that solve their problems, share their values, and care about them. That only happens when they are dealing with humans, not software.

Also, *stop selling*. People want to buy, not be sold to. If you create a compelling, authentic CPE, you will pull people to your brand. Think back on the 2016 launch of the $35,000 Tesla Model 3, Elon Musk's first affordable electric car. People lined up outside Tesla storefronts for blocks, and Tesla was not even selling anything. They were previewing the new vehicle and taking pre-orders. There were 375,000 orders, and the car will not even go into production until 2017.[6] But because Tesla's innovations have stoked buzz and the company has created a cool, high-tech dealership experience, customers turned out like they were lining up for a summer music festival.

Aha! does this by being transparent with our marketing. We show customers lots of screenshots of what we do, give them a fully functional trial account, encourage them to invite all of their colleagues to use it for 30 days, provide in-application demo data to explore, provide hours of how-to videos and pages of support documentation, and make it easy to get face time with a knowledgeable human who understands what they do about an hour after a request comes in. All that before they've committed to spending a dime with us.

Interaction Means Immediacy

But those measures would be worthless if we did not respond quickly when our customers ask for help. Response time matters. This is why we respond to all customer requests in under two hours. When people want human interaction, they have a real need that should be dealt with immediately. We have optimized our organization to provide expert support quickly at no additional cost. Pulling out all the stops to help our customers succeed is part of our CPE. We do not hide behind paywalls or time delays because that makes our commitment *conditional*.

We want our actions to send a consistent message: Our commitment to our customers' success is *unconditional*. We do a few hundred free demos a month for anyone who wants to attend. We have a fully public ideas portal at big.ideas.aha.io where anyone can provide feedback, see our product roadmap, and see what other customers are requesting. When support emails do not suffice, we initiate video conferences where we can show the customer exactly how to solve their problem. Technology and human interaction work together. That is not a cost. It is part of the product customers pay us to deliver.

> "People want to buy, not be sold to. If you create a compelling, authentic CPE, you will pull people to your brand."

You can scale and be human at the same time. Identify the moments when customers need to interact with a live person and then deliver interaction instantly and enthusiastically. The customer should not feel like an annoyance or an obstruction to your work. They should feel like the sole reason you are at work. Because they are.

Get Engaged

At Aha!, technology and people cooperate in a customer support process we call *intercept and engage*. This is where technology and people work together.

- **Intercept**

  We start by automating certain interception points. When we think a customer is likely to benefit from a human interaction but might be too shy to ask, we reach out to them and suggest a live support session. By itself, this wins us untold love and appreciation because virtually no one else does it.

- **Engage**

  When we get a request for help, we make sure the customer engages with a real person as quickly as possible. Because that person is real and authentic, he or she can talk straight about whether Aha! is a good fit for what the customer is trying to do. This is important even when we are telling customers what they do not want to hear. Some are taken aback at first when we say, "No, we won't implement your new feature request right now because it is not aligned with one of our core initiatives," but they all appreciate an honest response and a clear explanation.

Our Customer Success team members have deep domain knowledge. Many have done the customer's job at a previous company, so their practical, on-the-ground problem-solving knowledge is unparalleled. With this background and their expert knowledge of Aha!, there is a good chance that they can help the customer immediately on that call, avoiding costly, time-consuming support escalations.

Our customers tend to be product managers, so we need people who understand the challenges those customers face. I asked Melissa Hopkins, who leads the Aha! Customer Success team, to explain how the team approaches those challenges.

We have been in the shoes of our customers. We typically are hired in Customer Success because we've had success as product managers. We combine our successes as former product managers with what we know about Aha! and apply both with a consultative approach. If customers have a specific objective, we can combine what we know with what we've heard from other customers and how we've solved the same problem in the past to guide them to a solution. It's always a consultative conversation. Our customers feel that. When they ask us a question, we can give them best practices from other product managers . . . or we can think on our feet.

When (and How) to Scale

Companies have to grow, stagnate, or die. But if you prioritize value and personal relationships, when and how do you scale while retaining the kind of lovable support experience Melissa references?

When is easier than *how*. You scale if the immediate consequences for not scaling will be severe — if they will cost you customer love and even cost you customers. Aha! hired its first employee in March of 2014, about a year after we started. We had 125 customers and it was too much for only Chris and me to handle. We had clear product-market fit and knew we were on to something. People were telling us they loved what we were doing. We knew that it was our entire CPE, not just our product, that was earning such affection and we needed more people to keep delivering that CPE. We scaled the organization because not doing so would have hurt customers and our ability to create more value for more people. Our hiring policy is simple: We hire when it benefits customers.

How to scale comes down to communicating your organizational values and investing in training to make sure people understand them and know how to be guided by them. As soon as we decided to expand the team, we knew we needed to codify what was working and what was unique about Aha! We wanted to be able to share our approach with new people as they came onboard and build an organization that would stay true to the values that drove us.

When scale is truly necessary to grow your customer love, that is a critical tipping point for any emerging company. We did not want to move so quickly that we failed to create a framework for new employee success that ensured customer love would continue to grow. We wanted to franchise what we had learned and what already worked. Because our approach is radically different than the conventional wisdom, we knew from the start that it needed to be written down and injected into everything we did.

Our approach to customer success and the old-fashioned values that drive it combined to form what I told you a bit about — The Responsive Method (TRM). Our intercept and engage strategy, total authenticity with customers, immediate response to needs, abundance of resources available even to free-trial prospects — that is TRM in action in real time.

Five Qualities of TRM Hires

As we started to grow the team we also needed to define the qualities we sought in potential employees. We wanted to avoid a common mistake of scale-fast, scale-first startups: Hiring people for their skills without considering their character. We wanted people with deep experience and a history of success, but we also needed people who enjoyed making other people's lives better and who sought the chance to do purpose-driven work.

We defined a list of five must-have qualities that work well in any company built around TRM:

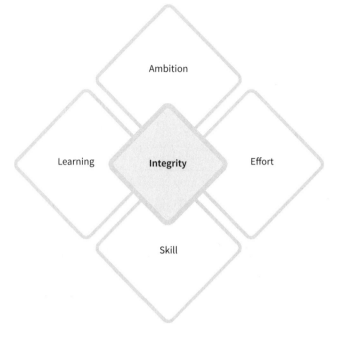

1. **Integrity**

   Every other quality on this list builds on integrity. Hire people of integrity — people who are as good as their word, respect others, and are driven by their own core principles. Fill your payroll with these people and they will give you everything they have — and your team will accomplish more than you ever thought possible.

2. **Ambition**

   If you are going to be a bear, be a grizzly. Go big. Look for people who set aggressive goals for where they'll be in three, five, or 10 years. Even if they cannot name the role they want in your company, they should be able to explain what excites them and the dream characteristics of their ideal job.

3. **Effort**

   A candidate once told me that "leadership is a born trait." I disagree.

Becoming a leader takes hard work. Doing anything with excellence takes hard work. Aspire to work with people who love accomplishment and are willing to work hard to achieve it in every area of life.

4. **Skill**

The more complex the task, the more training and experience you need to perform it well. In many jobs, you do not get a second chance. Education, experience, and ability to work well with others are important, along with the drive to keep learning.

5. **Learning**

Business and technology are moving too fast for employees to get comfortable. The best hires are open and committed to learning and embrace feedback. They should enable you to respond to changes with your customers, markets, and technology easily and without fear.

A Gentler, Saner Way

I have been hard on the "venture trap" approach to building a business, but it is still what most entrepreneurs dream of. Under the right circumstances, it remains a viable option and can result in some incredible companies. As I suggested, in industries where entrepreneurs need large, multiyear investments to generate innovative breakthroughs and a meaningful CPE, it is often necessary. Companies that depend on massive scale or customer acquisition to become profitable also need the big money that is only available through venture capital.

If that is what you need, go for it. Maybe you will be the next billion-dollar company. But beware the high-risk, high-reward game you are entering. Guard against collateral damage to your employees and yourself. Be aware of the traps of ego, hype, and self-delusion. Money is nice, but it will not build you a lovable product or bring you happiness.

On the other hand, if you are burned out by hype, volatility, and expectations, consider the grandpa-inspired approach we have taken at Aha! — a gentler, saner way to build a successful business. It is not as glamorous as raising $100 million, but it comes with a lot less negative human impact while being relatively immune to the trends and buzz that constantly buffet the high-tech world.

I have described how this approach, built on TRM, works well for software companies. But the same old-fashioned, relationship-first rules apply to building any technology-based product or service that does not inherently require a significant infrastructure investment. Think about your own product or service. TRM is likely applicable to you.

However, there is one realm of business where this approach does not work as well, at least not in its pure form — in large, well-established companies that try to broadly apply the principles. They need a hybrid approach. Big, slower-moving companies can benefit from a lovability mindset, but for it to have an impact they need dedicated resources and significant funding. In large companies, new projects have a small window to prove their worth and justify additional investment.

To build delightful CPEs, big businesses need hyper-focused teams that think and act like startups. They have existing revenue streams to fund new ventures and grade their potential against, so there is no need to take the slow, organic approach to growth. The "now or never" mindset that compels startups to risk it all to get big crazy fast can be just what the doctor ordered for large companies to get new initiatives to scale and to compete with current products within the company for resources and mindshare.

> "Be aware of the traps of ego, hype, and self-delusion. Money is nice, but it will not build you a lovable product or bring you happiness."

Get Connected

Seth Godin, the patron saint of change in the high-tech world, acknowledges that the winds are shifting for all companies. He writes that the Industrial Revolution of "better, faster, cheaper" is meeting a natural end driven by us, flesh-and-blood human beings. He suggests that the economy will be driven less and less by efficiency and more and more by what he calls the connection economy, in which people are valued both for their uniqueness and their ability to grow relationships.[7]

That is a healthier future. Growth might be slower but more real and more sustainable. If the new era takes hold, it will rebalance how companies are valued with an emphasis on fundamentals. It will also smartly discount flash-in-the-pan market hype and the potential of intellectual capital. For emerging technology companies, market hype and the perceived value of intellectual property have long been a strong force in valuation, but that may be changing. The value of deep customer relationships and profit and the opportunities they create are on the rise.

In today's world we still tend to value style over substance, but a new generation of more perceptive entrepreneurs seems to be learning from the mistakes of the past and applying more present-day wisdom. Hype is giving way to common sense. Because when the tide shifts, it's always real value creation — not deception or unsustainability — that bolsters valuation over the long term.

Grandpa-Inspired Benefits

The old-fashioned approach of our grandparents never went away. It just got lost in the glare of VC-backed superstars and flashy failures. It has rarely been sexy to write about companies that start small and grow slowly and organically over years, but maybe it is time for that to change. Those are the companies built to endure downturns — the ones that adapt to new trends, technology, and tastes, and serve owners, employees, and customers equally well.

Starting a business is not easy. For a variety of reasons, you might not be at a point in your life when you can do it. It takes financial stability and tremendous discipline, sacrifice, and a single-minded focus on achievement. However, if you are ready to build something that does not just build wealth for a few people but a better world for everyone it touches, here are some of the benefits of grandpa-inspired thinking:

More control

Despite the picture I have painted, most new companies are not built with venture capital. According to data compiled by business crowdfunding platform Fundable, only 0.91 percent of startups are funded by angel investors and 0.05 percent are funded by venture capitalists. So where is the money coming from? Fifty-seven percent of startups are funded by personal loans and credit and 38 percent by family and friends.[8] That is smart. While self-funding requires a lot of hard work and making tough trade-offs, it also gives you the freedom to do things your way, according to your vision.

When Craig Newmark launched what would become Craigslist back in 1995, not only did he not have outside funding, he did not even have a business plan. I do not recommend that, but he succeeded by creating something he cared about — an email distribution list in and around San Francisco — and posted it online. When it grew into a classified ad monster, investors pressured him to take their money. The company refused, waiting until 2004 to sell a 28.4 percent share to eBay. Craigslist Inc. has since bought back that share and continued to do things their way.[9] As far back as 2006, the company's president and chief executive Jim Buckmaster told reporters he was not interested in selling out, preferring to focus on helping users find apartments, jobs, and dates rather than on maximizing profit.[10] When you only answer to yourself, you can concentrate on building value your way.

FOCUS EXERCISE

Retaining control of your business allows you to focus on whatever is important to you. But do you know what that is? Fill in the blanks on these four statements to help figure out what you want to do and why you want to do it.

We will achieve ___*what*___ .
By this date ___*when*___ .
By taking these actions ___*how*___ .
For this reason ___*why*___ .

More independence

When you are independent, external pressures are less likely to keep you from following your vision. This is true for startups and established companies. As you know if you have worked in a big corporate environment, it is not uncommon for each stakeholder in a product to try to influence how it gets built, regardless of whether he or she is qualified to do so.

Charles Du designed NASA's first iPhone app, an award winner and a huge hit with more than 10 million downloads. But he also faced challenges from NASA brass who tried to water down his vision for the app. In a guest blog for Aha!, he laid out a basic principle: Maintaining your product vision is just as important as getting buy-in for that vision.

> After I got buy-in for the NASA app, a project manager was assigned to our team . . . a project manager is not the same as a product manager. Since my project manager didn't understand the difference between the two roles and had seniority over me, we fought many battles.
>
> The vision of the app was user-driven. So, I validated my product hypothesis by talking to users and looking at our website metrics — a user-centered design approach. The project manager took a different approach. She saw this app as an opportunity to get more resources for our local center . . . She was advocating for politics-centered design that was divorced from any customer conversations.
>
> To me, this is a clear case of why product vision should drive everything you do as a product manager. I had clearly communicated why the vision for this app would achieve NASA's high-level goals. This allowed senior leadership to see that I was working to help grow the whole organization. And it prevented politics from entering the picture.
>
> . . . We ended up launching a pure product designed 100 percent for our users — and it was a huge success.[11]

When you do not answer to special interests, you get to build the product that you envision and your customers love.

More discipline

When you have lots of cash on hand, you will be tempted to spend it — even when it is not yours and comes with crushing expectations. The burn rate — the rate at which a company's spending exceeds its income — for venture-funded startups is always higher than for bootstrapped companies because the money is intended to be spent to fund future growth. That can breed recklessness, and reckless spending kills companies.

Virtual assistant startup Zirtual raised $5 million only to abruptly shut down in August 2015. Former CEO Maren Kate Donovan explained that once the company switched from using independent contractors to hiring more than 250 new employees, the burn rate went through the roof. A hard-to-believe glitch in bookkeeping was blamed for failing to flag the out-of-control spending until the money was all gone.[12]

When you are responsible for every dollar, you watch every dollar and you are less likely to spend anything that is not absolutely necessary. You cannot have a burn rate for very long . . . because you do not have a lot of money in the bank to lose.

Bootstrapping forces discipline, and not just the financial kind.

More accountability

There is nobody else to depend on except for you and your team. While that might seem like a burden, it is really the gateway to success. No one achieves great things in their career until they master being accountable. Accountability is the opposite of hoarding credit when things go well or placing blame when they do not. Great leaders distribute praise eagerly, lead from the front, and accept responsibility when things do not go as planned.

At Aha! we are deeply accountable for everything we do and everyone we hire. We share accountability with the team by providing them with clear goals and templates for success. Each person knows their role and how they contribute to the team. Team leaders provide a backstop when something goes awry.

This philosophy is why we hire "full stack engineers." We do not have different engineers working on our software's back end, front end, and API. If you are an engineer at Aha!, you own a new customer experience from the back end algorithm all the way to the user interface. Our engineers may not be doing the designs, but they are accountable for the entire new customer experience — and fixing it if they got it wrong.

That kind of accountability is challenging but freeing. Instead of spending your energy on perception management, spin, and generating hype, you can invest it in making reality better.

More sustainability

The grow-at-your-own-pace approach lets you focus on profit before growth, so you can build something that lasts. You do not feel pressured to chase unsustainable growth to pump up valuation prior to your next funding event. In the software business, there are plenty of ways companies pursue unsustainable revenue growth, such as one-off professional service engagements, non-recurring engineering fees, and misaligned acquisitions. All boost immediate revenue, but they are distractions from the real work of creating lasting value, and each comes with severe opportunity costs, because the work rarely benefits all your customers.

With a sustainable model, you pursue what is most important to you within a company that helps you do that. Even in a larger organization, you can take steps to eliminate unnecessary customizations and get to more standard and sustainable offerings.

Sustainability is also about people. One of our chief goals in building Aha! was to create something that would be better both for the business and the people who worked in it. Our people work hard, as do the people in any successful company. But you can integrate your work into your life when your workplace enables you to live the way you want when you are at work and when you are away from it.

A sustainable organization respects the employee as the deliverer and creator of lovability and understands that you cannot foster love unless you feel it. It knows that for the employee, few things are more important than working and doing what is important to them. That's why we let our people work from home. I do it so I can see my wife and kids and ride my bike. I have played the role of the startup executive who spends every waking minute at the office. So has Keith Brown, who leads our marketing team. He managed a large team at one of the world's largest software-as-a-service (SaaS) companies but spent all his time on planes and never saw his wife.

Under a sustainable model, Keith's life is better. My life is better. Our employees' lives are better. Because they are happier, they stay, do great things, create more lovability, and make us more profitable. That might be an old-fashioned business model, but it works.

Matt Case, a team leader of our Customer Success team, said this about his experience:

> I had spent 15 years at the helm of various software products spanning supply chain, MES, and text analytics. I knew I was burned out. So, I chose to gain some clarity by humbly stepping away. It allowed me to became a much more central figure in my family's daily rhythm. I reconnected with my family in the best way — I spent more time with them. We traveled to Norway and saw places more beautiful than one can imagine. I also took on a few guest services jobs that had me on the ski slopes and rope courses of Park City, Utah. I gained immense pleasure by giving guests experiences to last a lifetime.
>
> But as time went on, I started to feel a void. I missed the adrenaline rush of working with innovative technology on products that helped solve hard problems. I missed working as part of a team to build something special. Just as I knew when it was time to step away, I knew when I was ready to return. However, I vowed that it would only be for the right opportunity that presented something special.

Matt joined Aha! in mid-2015: "My sabbatical from product management confirmed that I get the most joy when I am helping others. The Customer Success role at Aha! leverages my product knowledge to help my peers build better software and be happy doing it."

Lovability for Everybody

When my great-grandfather came to America, he was driven to create more value for himself, his future family, and the people he served. His life and business reflected that. We can all find inspiration in his vision of a better future and his self-reliant approach.

Now is the time to make the change to a gentler, more sustainable, more human way of growing a business. Start today. Implement TRM and those old-fashioned principles of relationships and service. You will see value right away. One of the benefits of TRM is that no matter the size of your company, if you are really operating in a way that puts people first, you'll know it. Customers will tell you in real-time what you are doing right and wrong. The feedback about what you are getting right will only strengthen your convictions.

If you're running a startup, give yourself an edge by building around TRM from the beginning. That will make it part of your company's DNA and give you an alternative path to build what you know is right. You will avoid the venture traps that lead many founders down the path to distraction, deception, and failure. Meanwhile, the extraordinary CPE you create will differentiate you from your competitors.

If you are leading an established company, you can take a dual approach to TRM. First, go big: Adopt it wholesale for new product offerings and make sure to properly fund them. Then, take the lessons you learn from those rollouts to gradually introduce TRM into your entire organization.

If that is too disruptive for your business, adopt a few ideas from TRM to start. I suggest being "interrupt-driven" and making quick interaction with customers your number-one priority. Even if you just take your support response time from 24 hours to six hours, you will still see benefits and customer love.

A great story about a big company's ability to do this comes from one of the world's biggest businesses, General Electric. I learned about Doug Dietz a few years ago when I saw him speak to a group of executives. Doug leads the design and development of award-winning medical imaging systems at GE Healthcare. He was at a hospital one day when he witnessed a little girl crying and shaking from fear as she was preparing to have an MRI — in a big, noisy, hot machine that Dietz had designed. Deeply shaken, he started asking the nurses if her reaction was common. He learned that 80 percent of pediatric patients had to be sedated during MRIs because they were too scared to lie still. He immediately decided he needed to change how the machines were designed.

He flew to California for a weeklong design course at Stanford's d.school. There he learned about a human-centric approach to design, collaborated with other designers, talked to healthcare professionals, and finally observed and talked to children in hospitals. The results were stunning. His human-driven redesigns wrapped MRI machines in fanciful themes like pirate ships and space adventures and included technicians who role-play. When Dietz's redesigns hit children's hospitals, patient satisfaction scores soared and the number of kids who needed sedation plummeted. Doug was teary-eyed as he told the story, and so were many of the senior executives in the audience.

Products should be designed for people. Businesses should be run in a responsive, human-centric way. It is time to return to those basics. Let TRM be your roadmap and turn back to putting people first. It worked for our grandparents. It can work for you.

WORDS TO LOVE BY

- **Lovability starts with knowing the reason you are in business**
  You must know the values and principles that guide you. It is the only way what you do will be authentic to the people you're serving.

- **Immediate interaction with customers is the key**
  When people want help, they want it now. How you react when they need you most says more to them about your company — and the character of its owners — than any marketing.

- **Old-school principles still work**
  Our grandparents and great-grandparents built businesses in a completely different way that centered on meeting people's needs. Lacking technology or venture funding, they saw a need, met it, and built trusting relationships over time. Aha! was built on those principles, and we should all return to those time-honored fundamentals.

- **Technology and cash are a curse for many entrepreneurs**
  Entrepreneurs wind up viewing customer interaction as an obstacle to business rather than its purpose, and chase hype and funding instead of building a profitable business.

- **It's possible to be efficient and human at the same time**
  Automate initial interactions but when people express a need for human interaction, drop everything and respond immediately. And stop selling. If you solve problems quickly and empathetically, you will not need to.

- **Hire your customers**
  To make an intercept and engage model work, you must have support people who have walked in your customers' shoes and know how to fix their problems.

- **Let The Responsive Method (TRM) be your guide**
  Following its principles makes it nearly impossible not to become more customer-driven, improve relationships, increase customer love, and have happier employees.

- **New hires for a TRM-driven organization need integrity**
  They also need ambition, effort, skill, and a willingness to learn. You need employees who are willing to put others first and who want to achieve something meaningful through their work.

- **Grandpa-inspired growth is not about feeling good**
  It delivers real benefits. Growing in this way gives entrepreneurs more control, encourages more discipline and accountability, produces companies that are more personally sustainable, offers a stronger path to innovation, and frees them to follow through on their vision.

- **TRM works for new and existing companies**
  It helps startups build organically and avoid traps, while helping established companies innovate internally by becoming more startup-like and creating real customer value.

Chapter Seven

THE RESPONSIVE METHOD

About half of all new businesses fail within the first five years.[1] The Responsive Method (TRM) is a proven way to improve those odds by providing a framework for benefiting from urgent interactions while remaining focused on your goals.

I have referred to TRM as a method or system, but it is more complex than either. A deeper analysis reveals three important aspects of TRM: *philosophy*, *interaction engine*, and *moral framework*.

Philosophy

TRM is grounded in the belief that sustainable, lasting success and happiness originate in the respect and service of others. The best way to attain your business goals, from consistent profits to personal fulfillment, is to do so indirectly by prioritizing other people's needs. TRM embodies time-tested wisdom that has become obscured in our modern age: The best business is *selfless* business. Lasting companies that benefit everyone they touch always place their values and relationship with the customer above hype, valuation, or ego.

Interaction Engine

Applying TRM requires a commitment to increasing the number of *urgent interactions* you have with customers. Urgent interactions are the key to TRM. They concentrate everyone's attention on personal, problem-solving communication.

People can contact your company with a question, a problem, or even something trivial and get a meaningful response with startling, gratifying speed. This tells the customer, "You are not an interruption of our work, but the reason we are here in the first place." In a time when some businesses use technology and systems as a means to distance themselves from their customers, urgent interactions are an effective way to differentiate your company and win customer loyalty.

Here is one example from a customer email that we received: "Thank you for pursuing and fixing this issue instead of ditching it in a bug-tracking list or idea bin (as many others would have done). It seems small, but to us this is a crucial feature and I am very pleased it was fixed that fast, great support!"

Urgent interactions must also be *quality* interactions. Employees should have the right knowledge on hand to make the interaction meaningful. This guided our approach to hiring former product managers to work with our customers. When someone has a question or problem, our goal is to provide an immediate response by someone knowledgeable who can address the question or solve the problem without delays or confusion. Usually, we can fix the problem or meet the need on the spot and customers are delighted. If we cannot answer their question or grant their request, the team has the skill and experience to explain why. This leaves the customer feeling appreciated and respected.

TRM makes it easy to be transparent, confident, and kind in all your interactions, because there are no hidden agendas. You can be generous with your time and assistance because both are integral parts of your product.

TRM reminds you that customers are people and encourages you to treat them all equally. At Aha! we treat trial customers, startups, and Fortune 500 companies with the same responsiveness and respect. People still ask sheepishly what we charge for training and consulting, and when we tell them that it is baked into the price, some are speechless, waiting for the "catch." There is not one. Others are shocked when we ask them to join an ad-hoc video meeting within minutes of their request to answer their questions and help solve any problems.

> "TRM makes it easy to be transparent, confident, and kind in all your interactions, because there are no hidden agendas."

With TRM, you get to know your customers like our grandparents once did. This makes it easy for both sides to share goals and ideas and find alignment with like-minded people. Because you are helping, not selling, you can be clear about what you believe in and quickly learn if the other person shares your values. In most companies, human interaction has been engineered out of the system. TRM makes it the heart of the system.

Moral Framework

TRM is also a moral and ethical stance that says you can live with goodness, treat others well, and still achieve great things, including strong profitability. Values, fairness, and caring about people are not *impediments* to profit. They are *instruments* of it.

Instead of turning employees' lives into the collateral damage of growth at all costs, business can enhance their lives, too. They will sleep well each night knowing they made positive connections and accomplished something meaningful that day. They will become better, more skilled, and more valuable as time goes on.

TRM has value to every type of company and every person within that company, but it is an especially potent tool for startups and emerging companies. When you are running a new business, you live on the clock. You have limited resources and time to make a meaningful impact in the marketplace — the kind that wins customers and produces profits. When every hour matters, TRM enables you to connect with more people, create more value, solve more problems, and win more loyalty. However innovative your technology might be, those are the human keys to a sustainable business that does good in the world.

> "TRM says you can live with goodness, treat others well, and still achieve great things, including strong profitability."

Great Product Managers and Asking Why

Sam Altman, president of Y Combinator, accurately said, "If you try to build a growth machine before you have a product that some people really love, you're almost certainly going to waste your time."[2] TRM is a system designed to address this problem — to produce not just great interactions but an outstanding Complete Product Experience (CPE). If you follow its precepts faithfully, provided that your team has the necessary skill set, a lovable product is a nearly inevitable outcome.

Begin by prioritizing and answering some difficult questions:

- **What are your goals?**
  Everything begins with goals. What are you trying to accomplish with your product? Why does it need to exist? Where are you headed and how will you know when you get there?

- **What customer problem will your product solve?**
  You need to be able to define the problem in a simple sentence. You should understand how often the customer faces the challenge and how painful it is. If that is clear, you will be able to describe what is needed to solve the pain.

- **What are your initiatives?**
  These are the big bodies of work that will help you solve the customer's problems and reach your goals. Initiatives are key themes that you will work on over time. They set the course you and your team will follow over a meaningful period.

- **What features are the highest priority?**

  If you understand your goals, the customer's challenges, and the high-level initiatives that will help you succeed, it is relatively easy to prioritize what capabilities to work on. But do not start here. Put your purpose and the customer first. If you do, the answer to, "What should we work on today?" will be obvious.

In most technology organizations, the job of answering these questions begins with the product manager. But too often, they start at the end. They ask about what technology is needed or what set of features will get the first version out the door. Unfortunately, those are not the right questions. Insights that will help you build an extraordinary CPE come from deep analysis of the reason you are doing the work.

Great product managers get primal when it comes to new ideas. They coolly ask, "Why are we building this?" *Why* is the most important question any product manager or company founder can ask. It is a holy word. Product managers understand that great products have a purpose that transcends their collection of bits. They ignore discussions of the bits until they understand why they are being compiled.

Great product managers also know that the only way to understand the *why* is to understand where the company is headed and the customers who will accompany it on that journey. To product managers, customers are on adventures of their own, but to reach their destinations and thrive, they need to get certain work done.

That framing device lets great product managers define the problems their product will solve and the functionality it will employ to solve them. With their deep customer knowledge, they can also identify and define the experiences that will surprise and delight the customer by meeting needs that customers either cannot articulate or do not realize they face.

Great product managers are stewards of your CPE. They think of new product versions not only in terms of direct value to customers but also how people will support the product and deliver the CPE. They know that salespeople have to be trained how to sell the product. Support people have to support it. Marketing has to position it and communicate its value. Finance has to bill for it. Everyone needs to share in the vision and goals of the new product so they can optimize its value for the customer.

Great product managers stay curious. They get a buzz from asking questions and understanding customer and team motivations. They get a shot of adrenaline when they solve a problem. They know that customers ask for new features because they need them to do important things. They understand that behind every request for a *what* is a *why*.

This is personal for me. TRM grew out of my lifetime of experience as a product manager at emerging technology companies. It grew out of thousands of conversations where I asked *why* because I wanted to understand a customer's true aspirations and motivations. I ask *why* because I care about time and what I can achieve with it. If you are passionate about solving people's problems and achieving meaningful things, *why* is the word that should open every conversation. You cannot get more time, so asking *why* helps you quickly get to the core of what matters most. Every time.

The Pillars of TRM

If you are drawn to hard work, meaningful outcomes, and testing the limits of your capacity, you do everything you can to put yourself in a position to succeed when opportunities present themselves. TRM is the framework that grounds me and our team in the methods we have used to achieve lovability and scale the company. TRM is our formula for growth, profit, and customer and employee happiness. Six pillars form the structure of TRM:

1. Goal-first

TRM is built on having a vision and measurable, time-based goals. Vision defines your purpose. It comes first. Goals are what you will accomplish and when. Together, your vision and goals are the *why* of creating a product and drive the *what* and *how* of engineering, code, and design.

Technology tends to emphasize a heads-down, incremental, iterative approach in which the product is nothing more than the sum of its parts. But to create a CPE that transforms your business, you cannot afford such reductive thinking.

If your plan is to build something of surpassing quality that people fall in love with, you must know why you are building it and why your customers will want it. This is your vision and you should be able to define it in a sentence. For example, at Aha! our vision is: *A world of better products and happier people building and using them.*

Goals are about having clarity on what you are trying to achieve. Having high-priority goals will help you achieve your product vision and business objectives. Goals should tie to your vision and be easy to understand, actionable, and achievable in three to 12 months. They must be measurable so you know when you have reached them.

2. Wow, curious!

We have a three-part approach to human interactions: *discover, motivate,* and *build.* When you discover, you are trying to understand what is important to the other person. When you motivate, you are trying to reach a mutually beneficial outcome. When you build, you are structuring a long-term relationship.

Because the process begins with discovery, curiosity is essential. Einstein said, "I have no special talent. I'm only passionately curious." Aha! employees are the same way; they are addicted to asking why and finding the answers. Curiosity is fundamental to learning and a leading indicator of success. If you are curious, you are interested and invested, so you will keep working at a problem until you solve it. At its best, work is a quest for knowledge powered by insatiable curiosity.

Curiosity is also an important tool for "surprise management." Relentless questioning can lead to positive surprises — discoveries — but it can also reduce negative surprises when interacting with customers. When you ask sincere questions, you discover what motivates your customers and what they want to accomplish. This ensures that intentions between both parties are aligned so everyone feels they receive full value for their effort and time.

Curiosity also helps people develop the empathy that is critical for lovable customer relationships. Empathy comes from understanding another person's situation — including their challenges and pain — and genuinely caring about them. You get there by asking sincere questions, finding common ground, and seeing the situation from the other person's perspective.

My cycling buddy, Joshua Lipp, runs a highly successful boutique contracts law firm. He is a great example of this. He is the only person I know who goes out of his way to ask to see potential clients' vacation photos when they rave about a recent trip. He loves connecting with his customers in this way, but it also gives him an unguarded glimpse of who they are and what they care about. That helps him serve them better. He believes people come first, which is what makes him a great lawyer.

Truly curious people like Josh and the best product managers I know do not fear being uncomfortable. Meaningful questions are a two-way street; if you ask, you must also be willing to answer. Building the kind of relationships that lead to a lovable CPE means letting yourself be vulnerable, revealing that you are not an expert in everything, and ceding control to the other person. When we are willing to be open and imperfect, we are at our most human, and that is when real connections happen.

3. Interrupt-driven

Interruption science insists that interruptions are always detrimental to human performance. But when you move from task completion to human relationships, interruptions are no longer obstacles to your work. Instead, they become opportunities to fix problems and make connections.

Reframing interruptions as valuable is what makes TRM possible. You start listening to what distractions are trying to tell you — someone needs your assistance. Customers are not trying to waste your time. They have a question only you can answer or a problem only you can solve. That is an opportunity to earn their trust and love. Being interrupt-driven means no longer cursing questions and problems as obstacles to work but seeing them as *the* work.

"When a customer asks for something with our software and it's easy to provide, instead of replying, 'Thanks, we'll schedule that for the future,' we'll do it right away," said Chris Waters, my co-founder. "They might be using that feature the same day. We interrupt what we were doing to deliver it. That's Continuous Deployment. With SaaS, you can provide updates to your customer within 30 minutes. But the willingness to be interrupted is an attitude, and it's unusual."

In an *interrupt-driven* organization, when people reach out with a need, other priorities are temporarily set aside. This might seem like a hindrance to productivity, but it actually redefines productivity. If the ultimate goal is lovability, then nothing is more productive than learning what customers want so we can make them happy. This approach also gives us an immediate feedback channel. By responding to a request or complaint without delay, we engage the customer before they move onto something else. This creates a virtuous cycle: We give them what they want, they give us instant and candid feedback, and we improve our ability to give them more of what they want.

Under TRM, all interrupts are created equal. Each is a potential opportunity for value exchange. However, they are created differently in that some create value and others do not. How you filter those is based on understanding your vision and goals. Goals are your filter. Without them, you will be overwhelmed by noise. If you know what your goals are, it becomes clear which interrupts merit a drop-everything, all-hands-on-deck approach and which are less urgent.

> "If the ultimate goal is lovability, then nothing is more productive than learning what customers want so we can make them happy."

At Aha!, we recently took this to the next level and committed to responding to all customer feature requests in one day. This means that when a request or complaint comes in, our product managers stop what they are doing, assess the request against our goals, and provide a meaningful response to the customer — even if that response is, "That is not in our plans." People will understand if your strategy is telling them "no."

Two words for startups about interruptions: Cherish them. When you are a new company you have few chances to interact with potential customers. Each is a chance to improve your odds for success and make your product indispensable. Be thrilled that someone wants to interact with you.

4. Yea or nay now

Yea or nay now is based on the principle that no one likes to wait and everyone hates to feel ignored. Your customers are happier when someone responds to them quickly, even if you are responding to say, "Sorry, I'm afraid we cannot help you with that."

All inquiries receive immediate replies, if only to let the person on the other end know their question has been received and that you will respond later in greater detail when you have information that will not waste their time. The goal is to impart the greatest body of valuable knowledge in the time available. That creates value for your company and your customer.

Yea or nay now is a framework that structures the chaos of building something and dealing with people. Ironically, it helps you stay focused and gives you back your time by uncluttering your world. By eliminating your communications backlog, you can concentrate on the present. It also frees up your time by giving you permission to do something many businesspeople fear: *Saying no to the customer*. Saying no is essential. It provides clarity and unclutters your mind to focus on your goals.

This approach also benefits customers. They need an answer or a resolution, and they will quickly learn whether you can help them or they need to look elsewhere.

Both yea or nay now and interrupt-driven contradict what you have likely been taught, which is that the only way to be productive is to minimize interruptions and compartmentalize everything. While that may be true for some employees engaged in high-intensity tasks, the opposite is true for people whose primary work is communication and relationship building. Ironically, individuals within many organizations waste more time on self-inflicted interruptions like checking Facebook and texting friends than they do on meaningful distractions like responding to a colleague who is trying to finish a time-sensitive project or helping a customer.

> "Your customers are happier when someone responds to them quickly, even if you are responding to say, 'Sorry, I'm afraid we cannot help you with that.'"

This approach imposes discipline and ensures that your team is getting the greatest value from their time. The more you and your colleagues practice responding instantly and resolving issues quickly, the more efficient with your time you will become (assuming that you hire the right people). That is what allows Aha! to support thousands of customers and more than 100,000 users with a small team while delivering valuable new software enhancements every week.

5. Transparent

With websites like Glassdoor.com giving everyone access to previously confidential information about pay, benefits, and work environments, it is becoming a competitive disadvantage to conceal too much about your business. While some things — customer information, source code, and operating plans — must stay under wraps, *transparency* helps create lovability's most crucial precursor: trust.

As Neil Patel, co-founder of Crazy Egg, Hello Bar, and KISSmetrics, writes in *Fast Company*, "Transparency produces trust. Who can trust a company or person who doesn't disclose information, who keeps everything close to the vest, who doesn't share anything? There are very few ways to build trust, but one of them is to be transparent. The opposite of transparency is secrecy, which only serves to erode trust."[3]

Consider Buffer, which makes social network account management software with more than 2 million users. Buffer has become as well known for its total openness about its revenues and employee salaries as for its product. It is a radical policy, but consistent with the company's stated values, the second of which reads, "Default to transparency." They have stayed true to this in good and difficult times.

There are two kinds of transparency — internal and external. At Aha! we make sure everyone in the company knows exactly what our goals are. We even train new employees in them and constantly share the major initiatives we are working on. Every Friday, we hold an all-hands company meeting and present detailed financials so everyone knows how the company is doing. That builds not only trust but confidence. It also drives accountability and makes it clear that we expect everyone to have a positive impact on the business.

In a public company, that kind of financial openness is more difficult. However, you can still remain transparent about goals, the success of initiatives, customer satisfaction, and other measurements of performance.

This openness is critical for anyone who wants to be a strong, effective leader. Transparency is a model for how you want your team to work. Sharing not only your goals but how you arrived at them encourages others to engage with you, challenge your assumptions, and make you stronger.

However, nothing is more important than transparency between a company and its customers. Secrecy encourages customers to create their own explanations for your decisions and policies — explanations that rarely give you the benefit of the doubt. Instead, when you answer a customer's question, explain the context. Be honest. Why are you telling them what you are telling them? If your explanation is well-thought-out and the rationale reasonable, they will respect the reason. Transparency leads to deeper, more productive conversations and greater levels of trust.

6. Kind

You do not often hear *kindness* referenced in a corporate context. Initially, it was not on our list, either. Then we realized that you could do everything else that was part of TRM, be wildly successful, and still be a jerk. The cost of being a high achiever should not be losing your humanity. I have always believed that it is possible to win, achieve success with dignity, and respect everyone (including people you do not agree with).

When I talk about kindness in business, a few people scoff. They say, "Steve Jobs and the leaders at Apple created a pressure-cooker environment but it produced category-defining products that people love and obsess over." That is the point — the results are not worth the cost, because there is an alternative. The goal of TRM is to create a kind, sustainable, and fulfilling experience for everyone. Caring and a sense of purpose evoke better performance than pressure and fear. The idea that only obsessive egomaniacs can produce breakthroughs is nonsense.

People are the most important resource for any business, and people — whether they are employees, vendors, or customers — respond best to kindness, respect, humility, and empathy. You never know what other people are going through in their lives. Many of us are under great stress, especially when business cycles shift and economic pressures build. Others are struggling in relationships. When everyone feels valued and heard, they are more likely to show up fully and bring their best each day.

Kindness is the alternative to the unnecessary "business is war" analogies that are not only tiresome but borderline offensive. It is the opposite of the "outcome justified the means" mentality that drives many entrepreneurs to consider sacrificing everything (including their morals) to build $100 million businesses in seven years. It's success without the collateral damage. This aspect of TRM creates a healthy framework for daily interactions and long-term goals and helps people avoid burnout even when they put in heavy hours over long periods of time.

We are all naturally optimistic, motivated to be better tomorrow than we are today. A kind organization understands that and leverages it. Your goal is to build a product that lasts, but to do that, you must also build an organization, a work environment, and a fabric of relationships that last too. People will remain engaged and focused on achievements when they are doing something meaningful that they care about in an organization that lets them live the way they want to live.

> "Caring and a sense of purpose evoke better performance than pressure and fear. The idea that only egomaniacs can produce breakthroughs is nonsense."

The Responsive Method

TRM is a radical new approach to personal and company growth.

Goal-first	If you are going to be interrupt-driven and respond to requests in real time, you need a way to assess the presented needs. You need to know whether you are going to invest real effort. And to do so wisely, you must establish a goal-first approach and a true north for where you are headed. A goal-first approach is about defining your vision and making sure everyone understands it.
Wow, curious	Einstein said, "I have no special talent. I'm only passionately curious." You too should be addicted to asking why and finding the answers. Curiosity is fundamental to learning and is a leading indicator of success. If you are curious, you are interested and invested, so you will keep working on a problem until you solve it. At its best, work is a quest for knowledge powered by insatiable curiosity.
Interrupt-driven	This is contrary to conventional wisdom, but we think that you and your company should be driven by interruptions. Most people are taught to try to tune out distractions because there are so many urgent but unimportant requests. Tuning them out is a mistake. Listen carefully to the noise so you can learn to pick out the valuable data.
Yea or nay now	You should respond to requests quickly because you cannot afford to keep revisiting them. You need to quickly analyze them as they are received and allow your goal-first strategy to guide you. The key is to digest the information and its importance as quickly as possible, so you can get on to the next one and creating more value.
Transparent	Explaining the "why" makes the "what" simple to digest. This is especially important when saying "no." The benefit is that if you share your assumptions and motivations and they are wrong, the other person will have a chance to help you see a better way. If you simply provide your answer, you are limiting your opportunity for growth.
Kind	People worry that being kind at work is often a sign of weakness. Nothing could be further from the truth. Being kind is good for you because it allows you to stay in control, remain humble, and maintain perspective. While it does not mean that you will always agree with everyone, it does allow you to stay calm and build strong relationships.

Sustainable Happiness

Following the six principles of TRM will result in an organization of people who reach the ultimate goal that I touched on earlier: sustainable happiness. The finest organizations make space for their leaders and employees to enjoy what they do well for years while enhancing each person's ability to find their own joy away from work as well.

Let me be clear again though — the goal is not work-life balance. Work-life balance suggests that work is a fundamentally unhappy state that only the other parts of life — travel, family, fitness, time at the beach — can remedy. But what if work were enjoyable and fulfilling, something that purposefully made you happy and filled you and your team with a sense of meaning and achievement? Sustainable happiness is about achieving what you want in your whole life, which includes what you do for work.

That is what you can accomplish when you use TRM to build products.

How TRM Empowers Product Builders

"With TRM, you treat people like peers," affirmed Keith Brown, who leads our marketing team. "It's important to realize that as technology enables information, the world is only getting smaller. Brian and Chris have a history of building great products and companies, so a lot of our customers are their peers: product builders serving product builders. With that kind of deep experience, we intimately understand the pain that these customers face. That comes first: Love and respect the customer. When you have that, you're being a good citizen of the world. We're all in this together."

TRM empowers product builders to get closer to their customers. It encourages them to be not only great businesspeople but their best selves. It turns gentleness, authenticity, and understanding into strategic assets and lets you prioritize and build what your customers value most. It frees you to use your passion and talents to create products that give your customers back their mojo and earn their love. That freedom is a world-changing tool in the hands of talented people responsible for deciding what they will build next.

TRM puts your corporate purpose on autopilot. It makes interactions more productive and kills distractions. By responding quickly, communicating clearly, and being transparent and kind, you minimize uncertainty and zero in on your end goals and broader vision.

Great product builders work best in an environment that they love and that loves them back. Aha! has used TRM to build that type of lovable culture, but the empirical benefits have been even greater. Our employee turnover rate is very low and two employees have even taken leaves of absence and returned. One employee left to build applications for the Bernie Sanders campaign (something we encouraged) and came back when the campaign wound down. And one employee left to build a high-profile mobile application for the Summer Olympics when his former company needed his help. He happily returned too. Productivity, morale, and retention are all off the scale. With studies estimating the cost of losing an employee as high as 200 percent of their salary,[4] that is a big deal.

Our revenue per employee is higher than that of larger software-as-a-service (SaaS) companies like Salesforce. We receive hundreds of customer Love Notes every month via Twitter, Facebook, email, instant messaging, and phone calls. Most gratifying, we currently have a 100 percent rating on Glassdoor.com with headlines like "Fantastic place to grow as an engineer!" and "Pioneering a new way to build customer relationships." Employees love what we have built with TRM, and happy employees create a lovable CPE.

How TRM Benefits Employees

TRM gives your team a sense of purpose, of doing something bigger than just working for a paycheck. TRM is a movement. It proves that you can build a sustainable, profitable business that is also good *for* and *to* people. As the backbone of your company, it will give employees a way to share the goodness in themselves with your customers — to be themselves, work the way they want to, be appreciated, and achieve great things.

Running with TRM as your operating system is not easy. As with any business, there will be ebbs and flows. There will be 12-hour days and intense deadlines. The difference in a TRM organization is that those challenging times have a purpose behind them. Without purpose, the weight of challenging work can slowly wear out some employees. With purpose, even weeks of late nights and tough problem solving are manageable because everyone sees the big picture and knows *why* they are working so hard. Purpose keeps morale strong when times are tough or rapid growth and scale put your capacity to the test.

I constantly tell our team, "You will look back with pride in five or 10 years and say, 'I helped build Aha! What we did was different. We changed how people built products and how they felt while doing it.' You will take those lessons with you and build your own companies and have your own great customer interactions. What you have helped create will be a transformational platform for yourself and the world."

People thought I was crazy when I started saying that, but our growth and fact that companies are asking us to train them on TRM are clear signs that the "movement" part is coming true.

TRM also makes it clear if someone is a good fit for your business, often before you hire them. That benefits employers, who waste fewer resources on people who will not work in harmony with the rest of the team, and employees, who learn quickly if they should seek a match elsewhere. TRM contains a beautiful contradiction: Be interrupt-driven but think big at the same time — respond to the noise but focus on the big picture. Not everyone is comfortable working in this way.

For the TRM-driven organization, a person's ability to engage in empathic, generous conversation and accept teaching and coaching is at least as important as his or her qualifications. A smart employee who gets TRM has a good chance of developing the elite skills needed to deliver an outstanding CPE.

"It's about fit and qualifications," according to Jamey Iaccino, who is a leader on our People Success team. "I enjoy being forward about the Aha! approach because candidates sometimes pre-screen themselves. There is a point in an interview where you can hear the person thinking, 'That's how I try to work, that's for me.' Or they'll say, 'I do not believe in being interrupt-driven,' and I'll reply, 'That's okay. We do.' When I was a recruiter in the past, I was selling. But at Aha! I identify people who not only have the expert skills we need but who also get excited about how we do things."

There is a risk: By helping people become the best they can be, you will lose some of them, and it will hurt. Suzanne Vaughan, a former member of our Customer Success team who you met earlier, left Aha! in 2016 to pursue her dream of becoming an executive coach. An inevitable consequence of building people up is that some will spread their wings and fly elsewhere. But you also have a deep bench of talent to step into the void because you're empowering employees to be their best and discover capacities they did not know they had.

TRM gives employees the ability to take joy in doing great work. As Paul Zuber of Thoma Bravo, who you met earlier, told me that is what we all want: "You spend so much time at work that you have to enjoy the people and should want to create great products that you will be proud of. Let's say you're a musician and you can only make 50 recordings in your life. Why would you create crappy music? Why wouldn't you want to build something great? Rather than viewing product as an outcome, treat it as a work of art."

How TRM Benefits Leaders

You might be thinking, "I do not have time for TRM." However, you do *not* have time not to take a new approach. TRM unclutters your mind and frees you to be your best. It is a methodology for product builders, executives, and owners who want to look back on the time they invested in their work with rewards and no regrets.

TRM reconciles the apparent contradiction between reacting to every distraction and staying focused on your broader vision — a notoriously difficult balance. It can be difficult to maintain a firm grasp of the big picture while simultaneously attending to the details of running an organization. In fact, a 2013 survey of nearly 700 executives across a wide swath of industries found that only 8 percent of top leaders were seen as excellent at both strategy and execution.[5] TRM gives virtually any leader a systematic way to think small and big at the same time and to turn that thought into constant, productive action.

It also adapts to the two most common entrepreneurial styles. Some entrepreneurs prefer to build frameworks from the top down and then get to the details. Others start with the details and then work their way up to a strategy. But what if you could do both? TRM begins with your goal and your curiosity and insights about it. From there, the details flow naturally based on interactions with employees and customers. You do not have to guess at what your customers want or the initiatives that will get you there — interruptions provide that information. With TRM, you will act on intelligence from the real world, filtered through your own values and experience.

TRM also gives leaders a framework for managing the messiness of building something and interacting with people. It reduces stress by eliminating the preoccupying backlog of unanswered communications and unmet needs. It gives you back your time by resolving issues and questions *now* instead of forcing them to play out over days. You will not be dragged down the rat hole by each person who interrupts you, but rather you will remain open to the disruptions so you can act on the ones that align with your goals and enhance the value of what you are creating. TRM enforces the disciplined time management that all companies — especially startups — need.

> "TRM gives virtually any leader a systematic way to think small and big at the same time and to turn that thought into constant, productive action."

Best of all, TRM is the cure for drama. I love clear plans and drama-free environments. I have even suggested creating "No Drama" badges for our team. Drama grows from hidden agendas, unkept promises, and a lack of transparency — all things that TRM quells. This does not mean that there is no stress at Aha! But our stress correlates with the value we provide customers and how much they love us. It is based on our high expectations of ourselves, and it serves the purpose of driving us to meet meaningful goals.

I have seen too much inefficient effort spent in organizations that are dysfunctional, unclear on their goals, and filled with conflict. TRM is a framework for healthy interactions and relationships. It is about putting your team in the best position for success — which puts you in the best position for success, too.

Yes, TRM Scales

As our company grows, I hear this question from customers and prospective employees more often: Does TRM scale? It seems logical that a personal, interrupt-driven process that works with thousands of customers would be ineffective and prohibitively expensive with 2 million customers.

In a conventional organization, where getting to know customers is left to marketing and technical support, that might be true. As John Peters, the CEO who you met in chapter 5, said during a conversation we had about building products: "You have to be anthropological to understand what a specific customer is doing with your product in order to see how it fits into that person's daily life. That's messy and expensive. Most companies are building products for end users they won't know. If your company is building products for doctors, but you're not a doctor, it's hard for you to build something engaging. You need to get to know them." That is true, but in a TRM organization everyone is responsible for understanding the customer and contributing to the CPE.

TRM is scalable in that it is a better way to build products and companies. It makes getting to know the customer at a deep level an organic part of how products are created and how companies operate. Every department, initiative, and communication is intentionally designed to gather knowledge about customer needs, shape product development, and drive the organization toward its goals. It disrupts industries in which customers have become second-class citizens.

I do believe the ultimate challenge for TRM is performing at scale. How big can it get? Can Aha! maintain the essence of what we have built with 50 employees when we get to 500? If we can do it at 500, what about when we reach 5,000? We believe TRM can scale effectively to those numbers and beyond, and we have already met with a number of large companies that are starting to adopt it. TRM is also an exciting experiment, and with experiments, there is always an element of uncertainty and learning along the way.

However, for a hint at how this one may play out, look at Google. They have nearly 70,000 employees, and they still hold weekly all-hands meetings that are broadcast live, where nothing is off limits and anyone can ask the founders a question.

Google explains why they hold this weekly open meeting on their website. "We strive to maintain the open culture often associated with startups, in which everyone is a hands-on contributor and feels comfortable sharing ideas and opinions. In our weekly all-hands 'TGIF' meetings — not to mention over email or in the cafe — Googlers ask questions directly to Larry, Sergey and other execs about any number of company issues."[6]

Google's example shows that TRM can scale up to the highest levels. It gives me confidence that we can do the same and have a massive impact on customers and employees on a global scale. It requires hard work, openness to thinking differently about how business is built, and a commitment of resources. But it is possible for every organization.

WORDS TO LOVE BY

- **The Responsive Method (TRM) is a method for building lovable products**

  You can do this by relentlessly prioritizing and constantly delivering an exceptional Complete Product Experience. It is also a powerful way to differentiate yourself from your competition.

- **TRM is a philosophy centered on happiness through service to others**

  It is an interaction engine that determines how interactions play out and lead to healthy, profitable relationships with customers. It is also a moral framework of success by helping people become better and happier rather than making their lives the collateral damage of business.

- **TRM is the tool of great product managers**

  Use it by asking four key questions: *What are my goals? What customer problems will my product solve? What are my initiatives? What features are the highest priority?*

- **Great product builders know that great products begin with purpose**

  Purpose comes from having a vision of the future and fully understanding customers — what they care about, what they worry about, what they need, and what delights them.

- **TRM is built on six pillars**

  Goal-first says that everything hinges on knowing the organization's vision and having clear, measurable goals. *Wow, curious!* says that an insatiable thirst for asking questions and learning about the customer leads to positive surprises while preventing negative ones.

Interrupt-driven says that interruptions from customers are valuable opportunities to learn and build strong relationships. *Yea or nay now* says that answering inquiries immediately, even if the answer is no, is the key to greater productivity and happier customers. *Transparent* is about openness, respect, and honesty. *Kind* takes compassion, respect, and caring and turns them into competitive advantages.

- **TRM benefits employees**

  It lends their work a strong sense of purpose. It gives meaning to times when work is challenging and exhausting. It creates a strong, distinctive sense of "fit" in an organization. And it helps people develop to the fullest, even if that means they move on from your organization.

- **TRM benefits owners and leaders**

  It reduces workplace stress and drama. It unclutters their minds and gives executives a tool for focusing simultaneously on the big picture and the granular details that are the difference between a good business and a great one.

- **TRM scales**

  It makes the constant acquisition of customer knowledge and the building of trusting relationships an inherent part of an organization's DNA.

Chapter Eight

HOW TO BUILD LOVABLE PRODUCTS

A lovable organization builds lovable products. It does so by delivering a Complete Product Experience (CPE) that customers and employees care deeply about. And as we have seen, The Responsive Method (TRM) is the system for discovering what customers need while creating the purposeful organization that can build it.

The advice and ideas in this chapter are the logical next step — the blueprint for applying TRM in real time. If you do, it will transform your business. You will be able to quantify the impact the changes have by measuring your lovability scores by using the tools featured in chapter 10.

My examples and advice will revolve around software businesses because that is what I know best. However, TRM and lovability are relevant to any technology-based product or service. And considering that every meaningful business today depends on technology to deliver a CPE, I believe that these insights and recommendations have widespread applicability.

Technology is already interrupt-driven — especially in the software-as-a-service (SaaS) era of endless iteration and instant updates. It is collaborative and dynamic in a way that no other industry can match. Whether your product runs on code or microchips, you can apply TRM to what you are doing to immediately do it better.

However, remember that the goal is not simply profit or growth but customer love. That means recalibrating how you see your business. Most technology companies are service businesses. More and more, today's technology is rented rather than owned. That makes it dynamic, changeable, and fluid — a model that benefits customers, who commit fewer resources to implement and support it while getting products that continually improve. This environment challenges product builders while shifting the power to customers.

For example, every year, I rent Intuit's TurboTax so I can do my income taxes. I pay for something I only need for a few weeks in February even though it holds my data for the entire year. That is because it has my data from the previous year (and for years before that). It simply asks if my financial situation has changed or if I have unique needs for a given tax year. It even has built-in, crowd-based support to help me when I get stuck. TurboTax meets many of the lovability requirements. It solves my problem, meets needs I did not know I had, makes my life easier, and adapts as my circumstances change. Best of all, I pay a reasonable price to rent it every year.

But how does Intuit really know what I need? Well, Intuit is famous for a program they call Follow Me Home. It sounds exactly like what it is — a way to observe customers in their homes or offices in order to understand how they actually use Intuit's products. The founding team used Follow Me Home as a way to help their teams get an immersive look at what customers liked and what they needed, as well as what worked and what did not work.

By observing customers in their own spaces, the Intuit team was able to see how often customers were interrupted while trying to use their product, or if they started on one device and finished the task on another. They were able to funnel that information back to their development team to make updates in subsequent releases.

It is important to note that they were not following customers home to look for bugs in the product. No, they had a deeper purpose — to truly understand the experience of their customers and if their products were making their work and life easier. That deep commitment to understanding customers helped Intuit find elegant ways to help them. It is a simple concept and one that more product builders would benefit from.

You Are What You Build

Technology pioneers understand that great companies invite their customers to help them shape what they deliver — to interact with their creative minds. They do not buy into the belief that the best products are built in silos or that theirs is the only valid vision. They grasp that the customer does not merely buy lines of code or a user interface but the company's thinking, processes, and attitude towards support and problem solving. In software, your CPE is a reflection not just of your team's skills but their values, passions, and character. You are what you build.

Ask yourself, "Who do we need to be when we are building product and delivering our CPE?" Lovability comes when employees bring their best selves to the table each day to solve customer problems and create delight — again and again. Each interaction with your technology, systems, and employees is an opportunity to build rich relationships and add value — to dramatically exceed expectations. Doing that will transform your products, process, and business.

> "Your CPE is a reflection not just of your team's
> skills but their values, passions, and character.
> You are what you build."

Delivering a lovable CPE also demands a higher level of innovation. Most company founders think of innovation as envisioning and inventing new stuff. However, it can also be how to improve each interaction with customers and your entire CPE. This kind of innovation reshapes organizations and how people do their work as much as the products they build.

Success Disasters

TRM's greatest power is its power to change how company leaders and employees *think* about innovation, relationships, interruptions, and customers. At Aha!, it has completely changed how we regard and prepare for potential problems. "Under TRM, we do not worry about every theoretical disaster ahead of time," said Chris Waters. He continued:

> If you have problems, you deal with them when they happen. Most people spend too much time worrying about the bad things that can happen due to success. Engineers will say, 'What if lots of people use our software and slow it down? We might not have enough servers!' That's a good problem to have. Plan for what is likely and do not worry about everything that might happen along the way.
>
> You can expend a lot of energy on things like that and the problems might never materialize, but the good things do not either because you were too preoccupied to make them happen. Fear carries a heavy opportunity cost. You can afford not to worry about unlikely problems ahead of time if you trust that you and your team can solve them when they happen.

We call good problems to have "success disasters," and we are delighted when they occur. When you have a responsive team and are confident in your skills, then mistakes and failures are golden opportunities to discover flaws in your process, build trust with your customers, and learn what they want and need with ever-increasing precision. Success disasters are not judgments — they are incentives to continue pursuing greater achievements.

The fluidity with which failure and recovery occur is what makes TRM so well suited to building software and other technology products. Back when a product was defined by its array of manufactured molecules, changing or updating it was time-consuming and costly. A single failure could wreck a business. Products built on bits are dynamic and the methods we rely on to build them are changing. Before, we could not quickly take customer ideas into account. Now, we cannot succeed without doing so. Changes in the marketplace, customer demands and education, people's ability to gather information — they have gone from being headaches to being essential parts of building lovable products.

Building great products today is about interaction and information. We are interacting with customers as never before via social networks, email, support forums, and more. The amount of information and opinions written and published about technology is unprecedented. Do you use this flood of information and interaction like a power source that fuels great products, or try to paddle upstream against it and build great products in spite of it? We have chosen to do the former, but it's impossible without a framework. TRM is an interaction and information-gathering framework — a *relevance* framework. It helps us ensure that we listen to the customer feedback and ideas with the greatest value and that what we build is relevant to the people who need it so that they can do important, meaningful work.

> "Fear carries a heavy opportunity cost. You can afford not to worry about unlikely problems ahead of time if you trust that you and your team can solve them when they happen."

Using TRM to Build Products

TRM defines more than just how we work at Aha! It defines our values and the principles we use to build products. This section describes how we put those principles into practice every day. Keep in mind that I am not talking about using TRM to build a lovable company. (That will come in the next chapter.) But everything begins with the delivery of a CPE that earns customer affection and loyalty. Without it, no one will love your product or company.

While TRM is a proven framework for lovability, it is not the only prerequisite for success. You still need a team of talented people, a strong process for turning ideas into achievements, and the resources to do the job. If those are the price of admission to build a functioning business, then TRM takes you to the next level — to a thriving product and a great business.

TRM can also have a positive impact on developing nontechnology products and services. Most industries could benefit from improved responsiveness, happier workers, and greater knowledge of their customers. The following list explains how to put TRM to use and is oriented for technology products, but I invite you to experiment and adapt these methods as you see fit.

Think and feel (get inside the pain)

TRM starts with empathy — understanding what the customer is thinking and feeling and why. You already know that we do not have traditional sales and support people. It's why we onboard all new hires at Aha! as honorary Customer Success team members so they meet customers and understand their pain. It is a way to institutionalize empathy both for customers and each other. Over the month-long onboarding process, engineers, marketers, people success and finance managers, and all other new team members learn how challenging product building can be because they work directly supporting our customers.

To have empathy for your customers, you need to have lived their lives. You need to know what inspires and vexes them before you can help them. If you do not deeply understand your customers today, figure out a way to follow them home like Intuit does (with their permission of course). Spend a lot of time with them on the phone, on videoconferences, and in person. Learn what they care about and what they fear. Map out the challenges they are experiencing and the journey they are on with your product and company. Understand them better than they understand themselves.

Customers will be surprised that you are engaging them so personally and authentically. Some might not know how to react, especially if their general customer support experiences have been impersonal and unsatisfying. Research shows that helping others makes us healthier and happier, and at Aha! we have found that empathy for customers makes helping them an enjoyable experience.

Melissa Hopkins, who you met earlier and who runs Customer Success at Aha!, said that at first, being responsive and immediately helping others becomes so pleasurable that new Customer Success team members have to remind themselves to slow down. "You can get so caught up in watching support requests come in and going after them immediately that you have to remind yourself to breathe and eat," she said with a laugh. "We hire people who are interested in helping customers because it feels awesome. We don't worry about creating high expectations because we *want* customers to have the highest expectations of us."

An environment where employees derive pleasure from solving customer problems may sound idealistic, but it is both sound business practice and crucial for lovability. The peak-end rule is a psychological heuristic that states that most people judge an experience based on its peak — the point of greatest intensity — and its conclusion. For most of your customers, their peak intensity moment will be when they need you to help them solve a business-critical problem . . . or perhaps just save them from frustration. Do you care enough to help them when they need you most? Are you connecting with them by understanding their pain so that even if you cannot solve their problem, they leave feeling heard and respected?

Your team will only go to those lengths if they know your customers, care about them, and find common ground.

First one focus, second one free

As I mentioned before, I ride my bike several times a week and use the Strava application to track my distance and speed and compare my workout with other cyclists in my area. The app is a terrific example of a company doing one thing extremely well. So I was surprised in 2014 when Strava made a deal to sell its dataset to the Oregon Department of Transportation to be the data backbone of a Portland bicycle-use planning project.[1] The deal was understandable considering the hype surrounding Big Data and the massive dataset that Strava had accumulated, but a dual-market strategy rarely works for emerging companies.

I do not know how well Strava is doing from selling crowd-sourced data from people like me. But I do know that splitting market focus often divides an organization because it requires a totally different mindset and business model. The problem is that when you try to focus on a second strategic product initiative before you have traction with your first, you increase the risk of failure for both. It is a bit like what happens when you try to juggle one more ball that you are capable of juggling — you drop all of the balls.

It is critical to do one thing well and continue until you do it brilliantly. If you get it right and you build something lovable, you will find opportunities to expand and serve different types of customers. That is what I mean by the phrase "First one focus, second one free." Excellence drops your second opportunity in your lap. But if you do not achieve excellence with a primary product first because you divide your focus, you will not get a second opportunity.

Chris and I learned this building our previous companies and watching other people build theirs. Building a business makes you insecure. You second-guess yourself. You worry that what you are doing is not big enough, innovative enough, or important enough. These concerns influence many product builders to start trying to add more value by creating new products, adding new features, launching new programs, or seeking new partnerships. However, by introducing more activity you make it harder to realize true accomplishment. You dilute your time and talent.

Growth for any young company is essential, and we all want to build something that grows and thrives. At Aha! it would have been easy to divide our focus if we had not been careful. We provide SaaS for businesses that need to set a business strategy and create a product roadmap. From day one, we focused on companies that were building software or software-enabled products or services themselves, but our product could apply to a lot of other use cases. In our second year, we asked, "Should we pursue additional revenue streams where we are seeing customer traction, or stay focused on the core business that has served us so well?"

After some deliberation, we explained to the team that we were going to double down on our core market and improve how we served product managers. Other customers might be buying Aha! for a wide array of strategic planning and roadmapping needs across many different industries, but we knew it would be best if we stayed true to our initial direction.

That was the right decision. In 2016, we grew our revenue and number of customers by more than 100 percent and doubled the size of our Customer

Success team, and we did it all profitably with no outside investment. It takes discipline and courage for a rapidly growing company to do this.

If you are thinking about detouring from your established path, proceed with caution. When meaningful people come to you with real opportunities that lie just outside of your sweet spot, take a hard look at your goals and how you will reach them before you change direction. When in doubt, stick with what you do best and say, "No thanks, maybe later when we gain unquestionable traction in our primary market."

Prioritize everything

Increased choice and improved quality are leading customers to see technology products as interchangeable. Because of this, customer loyalty is at a low ebb. At first glance, building new technology appears to be linear and hierarchical, with one stage or feature leading to the next. But when you are creating something holistic with the goal of delivering delight to your customer, every aspect of the customer experience is critical. Everything you work on must be a priority.

This approach starts with strategic goals. If you have strategic goals, it is easy to create a series of high-level actions that will allow you to achieve them. We call those *strategic initiatives*. Strategic initiatives link directly to your goals, guide what you work on, and shape where and how you choose to invest your time. If it is not strategic, do not work on it.

How do you know if an initiative is strategic? In our software development process, discrete work items are called *features* or *user stories*. Our tool includes scorecards that you can use to continually score how closely a given piece of work relates back to your strategic initiatives. This allows you to attend to the details of building your product while also maintaining a high-altitude look at your work and determining what will have the most impact on your business. That is how you know if your day-to-day work is strategic.

We call it the "red thread of strategy." Broad-based strategic thinking should tie everything you do together with the bigger objectives you are trying to accomplish. The decisions you make from the bottom up should tie into your top-level goals. You can see how everything becomes goal-driven. When you operate this way, an audit trail runs through your work (like a highly visible red thread) and keeps you on point towards your larger goals.

We recommend you build a table like the example that follows to help visualize your goals and initiatives and map them to the work your team does on a day-to-day basis:

⚑ Strategic Goals	⛩ Strategic Initiatives	📅 Product Releases	▦ Product Features
Fredwin Software Goal			
	Fredwin Software Initiative		
		Fredwin Software Release	
			Fredwin Software Features
Grow marketplace to over 500 partners in the next 18 months	Build next-generation partner portal	Partner portal 3.0 winter launch	Improve partner sign-up process
			Automate welcome emails
			Allow partners to custom brand the site
			Support credit card payments
			Enhance analytics

Strategy is not random. "The boss woke up on his left side this morning and decided we should start doing more of X" is not a plan. But while strategy is essential, it is not inflexible. If the underlying assumptions that it was based on change, so should your strategy. Product managers will sometimes say, "There's nothing I can do; this is what the strategy says," as a justification for dodging ideas and impulses that can knock them off course. Strategy must adapt as needed to bring you closer to your goal.

As Shardul Mehta of *Street Smart Product Manager* wrote on the Aha! blog, "There are many prioritization techniques out there: scorecarding, the Kano model, etc. Basically, prioritization stems from the product strategy and the company's strategic focus. For example, if the company is in major growth mode, things that help drive customer acquisition may be prioritized first. If the primary goal is driving revenue via penetration of the existing customer base, then initiatives to help accomplish that goal may be prioritized above others."[2]

As long as the goal is visible in the window, strategy has the final say. The plan always dictates what has priority *now*, with everyone understanding that as the conditions change, the priority may change.

Prioritization also helps you avoid over-committing yourself or your team. Your product strategy dictates what is important. It also provides a framework for everything from how you manage new product releases to why you consider some customer ideas over others. This is your chance to captain the product's ship — not to try and please everyone. The "red thread of strategy" should tie all of the work you do to exactly what you are trying to accomplish.

Differentiate everywhere

According to 2013 consumer research by NewVoice Media, 44 percent of U.S. consumers switched to a competitor following a poor customer service experience — 53 percent because they felt unappreciated. Fifty-three percent also think that a phone call is the most effective way of dealing with a problem and 33 percent prefer to address issues via email, but more than half say they are irritated if they do not immediately speak to a real person. NewVoice data also shows that 50 percent of consumers will use a company more frequently after a positive customer experience.[3]

In a world where your product can be viewed as a commodity, you do not deliver a product. You deliver a CPE. You use every touch point with your customer to let them know that your business model, people, philosophy, and culture are unique and worth paying a premium for. Use every encounter as a chance to differentiate your business from its competitors.

Everyone in your company who interacts with a customer leaves a unique fingerprint. Collectively, those interactions create the customer journey and, ultimately, how your customers perceive you — your brand. Each interaction is an opportunity to drive home the message that your CPE is like no other.

The Aha! approach to customer communications surprises and delights people. We handle tens of thousands of customer support requests a year and respond to all customer inquiries from anywhere in the world in an average of two hours. That does not mean a canned email, but a personal response from a knowledgeable individual capable of solving the problem. Our first-time close rate on customer support requests is close to 60 percent as well. That tells customers more about our commitment to them than any advertising initiative. Action always speaks louder than marketing.

However, we also send carefully crafted emails to customers after they sign up for a free trial, proactively welcoming them, offering help, or suggesting best practices. This is not selling. It is us acting on behalf of our customers, caring about their experience, and respecting their time. We go to great lengths to optimize our written communications to help customers get the most out of our talented team. One example:

> Hi Steve,
>
> I am contacting you again because you recently signed up for an Aha! trial. Unfortunately, it looks like you have not been able to spend much time getting started.
>
> I am hoping to better understand why, because we are working right now to make it easier for customers to get started.
>
> Can you respond and tell me how we could have made it easier? We would also be happy to give you a demo if you are interested. We are a company of former product managers.
>
> Do you have time next Tuesday or Thursday?
> Thanks,
> Brian

Many technology companies view communication with the customer as a necessary evil and engage in it grudgingly. We do the opposite. We go out of our way to initiate interactions with our customers and spend time in meetings with them. Each is one more chance to show them that Aha! is different, understands them, cares about solving their problems, and is willing to earn their loyalty. We are a group of knowledgeable and talented people serving the same.

Intercept and engage

I introduced you to this concept in chapter 6. It is not uncommon to find leaders who view human contact as a cost center rather than the reason they are in business. They practice "contact avoidance," deferring human interaction whenever possible through automated phone systems, online knowledge bases, peer-to-peer support forums, and the like. These measures send customers a clear message: *You are not important to us.*

You cannot build a thriving business that earns customer love by dodging customer contact. Instead, businesses of all sizes (particularly startups, which must get it right) should go out of their way to create human interactions — to intercept customers at the moment of their greatest need and engage them in a meaningful way that fulfills that need.

I have already explained why we welcome interactions with customers at Aha! We initiate them, especially in situations where we think people are too shy to ask for help. After speaking with thousands of customers and learning where they typically needed a bit more help or encouragement, we identified a pattern and began reaching out at those critical moments. That has helped them get more value from our products and led to intense, consistent customer love.

We also invert the common role of technology in support communications. In almost every technology company, a customer who contacts support will first find themselves pointed toward a searchable knowledge base or receiving a chain of impersonal emails from someone unfamiliar with the product but paid to try to solve their problem.

We do the opposite. We use technology to automate the intercept and then insert people into the conversation. If you set up a trial, you will get proactive communications from people on our team who have successfully built software. Forget email fatigue. A significant percentage of our customers respond to our emails because they want to speak with a real person who is just like them.

We have nothing against support technology. If you can get the answer to a question from watching a video, great. But our goal is to provide a surprising, gratifying, lovable CPE, and the best way we know to do that is to make human interaction a priority, not an afterthought.

This is also when we subtly let people know that Aha! does not have sales-people. Our Customer Success people will respond to a support request or start a demo by explaining, "I'm a former product manager, and my purpose is to help you get the most value out of our product." There is never a sales pitch or an upsell.

Not a single person receives commission-based compensation at Aha! When customers learn that, they relax. They know they are being treated like people, not a means to someone's fatter bonus. We can have richer conversations knowing there are no hidden agendas.

If you decided to pilot this type of customer interaction, how would you know if it was working? You could look to sales and traditional customer satisfaction surveys, but instead, start tracking your lovable interactions. We share them internally through our group messaging tool in a channel that we call #lovability, where employees can share their lovable customer engagements with the whole team. We track the velocity of lovable interactions on a quarterly basis. It is also a fun morale booster that reminds the entire team why we all work so hard, and it binds us together from our remote locations. A few examples . . .

- *This is the greatest thing ever: Product managers helping other product managers!*

- *Aha! frees people up to do the parts of product management they love.*

- *You guys are awesome. We were wishing we had this feature literally this week for product steering. Now we do. Keep up the good work!*

- *There are people in my organization who will cry (tears of joy) when they see this.*

- *My team uses Aha! and bloody loves it!*

- *I think your product is an absolute dream that I wished I had access to years ago.*

- *Best customer support, ever!*

It is humbling when innovators in organizations around the world reach out to us to express their gratitude in such honest, effusive language. All we can do is our best and hope that people appreciate what we are giving them, and so far, they do.

Those messages reflect a subtle but important purpose behind our work. Being product builders ourselves, we realized long ago that no product manager enjoys everything about building new products. Part of a lovable CPE means that we can help our users be brilliant at the parts of the task that they enjoy while making the parts they do not enjoy easier.

Think about how you view sales and support. Are you offering support willingly and enthusiastically? That is a powerful predictor of lovability. If you are not working on an intercept and engage model, perhaps it is time to ask yourself how customer support can become not a cost line item but a tool for building profitable relationships.

Ship, ship, ship

Seth Godin writes with his usual wit and eloquence about overcoming the fearful "lizard brain" to be a successful purveyor of products:

Ship often. Ship lousy stuff, but ship. Ship constantly.

Skip meetings. Often. Skip them with impunity. Ship.

Trick the lizard if you must, but declare war on it regardless. Understand that the only thing between you and the success you seek in a chaotic world is a lizard that figures out that safe is risky and risky is safe. The paradox of our time is that the instincts that kept us safe in the day of the saber tooth tiger and General Motors are precisely the instincts that will turn us into road kill in a faster than fast internet-fueled era.

The resistance is waiting. Fight it. Ship.[4]

I disagree with "ship lousy stuff," but the rest is right on. Any time we can do something small with our product to create delight, we do it. Immediately. This is easy in a SaaS environment because we can update our product instantly, but it also requires the will to ship and ship consistently.

We ship whenever a new feature has been finished and tested. We have conditioned our customers to expect a meaningful new product feature every Wednesday. They actually get more, but we announce something new every Wednesday. We announce it via a message presented right in the application and include a link to a blog post that describes what it is, why it's useful, and how it works.

This is like getting something special in the mail. Back in the days before Amazon and digital downloads, there was Columbia House. Remember them? You would get a card every month showing you all the new music you could buy on CD (or cassette, or vinyl if you are old enough) and you would send the card back telling the company which records to send you for $5. Then you had weeks of delicious anticipation waiting for your new music from U2, The Clash, or AC/DC. We try to give our customers that same little *frisson* of anticipation, and we do it at no additional cost. All product improvements are baked into our base service fee. They are a gift for being a committed Aha! customer. They also reflect our understanding that all software is rented today. It must keep getting better.

In the past, technology builders worried that shipping more often led to more problems. Or that they could not have a meaningful plan aligned against strategy and still ship, ship, ship. Not true. Shipping fast is consistent with having a clear plan and typically reduces risk. There is less that can go wrong and it is easier to isolate and fix problems if they do occur. We use publicized weekly product launches as one more way to create delight and elicit useful customer engagement.

Building and shipping fast is part of our DNA. We are allergic to boredom. We want to ship new things and we get ornery when we do not. We even look for this kind of creative restlessness in the people we hire.

Stop to smash bugs

TRM means being responsive to everything, including problems. When a customer informs us about a bug in our software, we drop everything to discover the nature of the bug, fix it, and post an update. Stopping to smash bugs is a big part of what makes us who we are. Customers love us for it. After we fixed a bug that he reported *one hour* earlier, one customer wrote to say, "When you fix shit that fast, there is no need to apologize."

This circles back to being interrupt-driven. Interrupting work to fix problems is a lesser evil than creating technical debt. Technical debt (which I referenced in chapter 2) reflects the extra work that arises when engineers use code that is easy to implement in the short run to address an issue instead of applying the best solution. However, you create a more insidious debt when you let bugs proliferate.

Technical debt accrues in unresponsive companies because they do not commit to fixing bugs. The problems quickly appear insurmountable, and they give up. That is a shame, because they could have used timely fixes and updates as additional chances to earn customer love. Instead, technical debt becomes a burden for customers and employees, because humans cannot keep track of everything that does not work. They learn to work around it — or worse, become blind to it. Software engineering at the highest levels requires incredible intellect and concentration, and if bugs are not squashed immediately, they linger, multiply, and grow.

Every interaction a customer has with a bug diminishes their experience and your lovability. If you are following TRM, it is your responsibility to reduce those annoyances as quickly as you can. What could be more important?

TRM companies take the same approach to customer ideas and feature requests. Talk about fertile ground for idea exchange and information gathering! We encourage our customers to send us their thoughts and ideas for improving our product, no matter how seemingly trivial, because we do not have all the answers. Customers know better than anyone what will make their jobs easier and their lives better.

We also have an active ideas portal at big.ideas.aha.io where customers can suggest new functionality or feature improvements to our roadmapping software and vote on what they think we should prioritize. We have received more than 4,000 ideas so far, ranging from a request to improve how we provide resource capacity planning, to a proposal for a single daily email digest, to a list of additional systems that we should integrate with. We are unique in how we treat these ideas. Each one is precious to us and we have a "zero unreviewed ideas" policy. (Seriously.) We review each idea as it comes in and prioritize the ones that align with our goals and will have the largest impact with the least effort.

"Customers tell us that they are interested in mimicking our process and communicating with their customers using the same responsive process around ideas," said Melissa Hopkins. "They want to tell their customers whether or not they plan to use the ideas coming into their own portals the same way we do with ours."

Get real

That continual flow of interactions, questions, and solutions reminds us of something no business can afford to forget — a corporation is simply a legal fiction. The company does not do anything. People do. Please do not ever write "the Company" in a document, whether it is an annual report or an HR manual. The only capital letters in your documents should appear at the beginning of people's names.

If you want customers to love your business, be authentic. Authenticity is relevant everywhere and every day. It starts with being confident about why you are in business in the first place. You should explain your motivations when asked. You are in business to create customer value and the only way to continue to provide more of it is to get compensated for what you do. Making money is an important aspect of what you do, and it is perfectly acceptable to admit that. Just be equally clear that the way you plan to make money is to help the customer in any way you can.

You also need to make real connections. Technology may be a huge part of our lives but we still crave human connection — perhaps even more now because so many of our interactions seem to occur online. Something as simple as asking a personal question about how someone is doing or sharing something about what you did over the weekend can set you apart. So can admitting when you have made a mistake and going out of your way to make it right.

You will not be able to make all of these connections yourself. Everyone in the organization needs to be comfortable being authentic. Trust your team. If you do, your customers will trust them too. Some companies confine employees to smaller and smaller areas of responsibility as they grow, but that only teaches them to doubt their abilities. Train them to answer more questions with greater confidence and model that behavior for them.

> "Trust your team. If you do, your customers will trust them too."

Finally, help the team (and customers) by doing away with unnecessary hierarchies. Hierarchies create abstraction and kill authenticity. Allow relationships and communication channels to flow naturally throughout your organization. Get comfortable with your own role in the organization and the value you provide. Take ego and friction out of how people work together. Sometimes, that means that you need to get out of the way to help people themselves.

Give, give, give

Social networking and marketing consultant Peter Shankman tells this astonishing customer service story. Back in 2011, he was flying from Newark to Tampa for a meeting and then back the same day. By the time he reached Tampa airport for his return flight, he was starving. A steak lover, Shankman jokingly tweeted at Morton's the Steakhouse, asking the chain to meet him at Newark when he landed — with a porterhouse steak, of course.

When he landed, his eyes scanned for the driver his assistant had arranged to take him home. He found the driver holding a placard with his name on it. But as he approached the man, he noticed another fellow standing beside him. And this man was holding a bag from Morton's. Inside? The steak he asked for, along with all the fixings. The Morton's representative simply said to Shankman, "I heard you were hungry." Needless to say, Shankman was floored.[5]

This story went down in social media history as one of the all-time customer service exchanges. But since 2011, a few other companies have added their names to the list.

A woman staying at the Gaylord Opryland resort in Nashville, Tennessee, so enjoyed the "spa sounds" feature on the clock radio in her hotel room that she tweeted the hotel asking where she could buy one. She was disappointed when they informed her that it was a custom soundtrack not available for purchase. But when she returned to her room she found a brand new "spa sounds" clock radio to take home, along with a handwritten note from the staff.[6]

Or how about the young boy who saved up for two years to buy a LEGO train set — only to learn that it had been discontinued and was a collector's item far out of his price reach. The boy, who has Asperger's syndrome, was part of a LEGO playgroup that helped bolster his social skills. He wrote a letter to the company asking if there were any left at their corporate offices and, if so, could he purchase one. Not only did LEGO gift him the discontinued set, but they sent a detailed letter encouraging him to never give up on his dreams. (The unboxing was captured by the boy's parents on a hidden camera and posted to YouTube, to viral effect.)[7]

That is creating customer delight. You do not need to go to such extremes, but to make a point internally, maybe you should. What are some outrageous ways you could make life better for your customers? They do not have to be dramatic; small things make a big difference.

For example, online bank Simple is well-known for its quirky, personal customer communications, and one of its most popular came when they put their own spin on those boring privacy policy updates and regulation guidelines that banks have to send from time to time.[8] They simply decided to "translate" one of those communications into ordinary English running alongside the federally required legalese, including silly passages like this:

> Translation: There might actually be rare cases when you have to write us a letter to officially document fraudulent activity on your

account. A real letter, like, on paper! If this happens, it will probably be the first real letter we've ever received at Simple. Exciting! To commemorate the occasion, we promise to write those first 50 letter-writers back, by hand, using our fluffiest feather quill.

That email received lots of quick, enthusiastic feedback. The lesson: Give your customers the kind of experience you wish other businesses would give you and pass along some unexpected joy.

Report on progress against measurable goals

Remember that everything comes back to your goals. Each of the prior nine principles is important, but it is also important to periodically check the map to make sure your business is on course, and to course-correct if necessary. You should consistently be planning, working, and measuring to be your best.

This list is specific to SaaS products and companies and represents a sampling of possible metrics you could use. If you are not building SaaS or software, use these as inspiration to help you choose what to measure that will give you a clear picture of your progress:

- **Monthly unique visitors:** Traffic to your website.

- **Customer acquisition cost (CAC):** What you spend in marketing divided by the number of new customers that sign up.

- **Organic traffic vs paid traffic:** Traffic that comes to your website due to marketing, SEO, word of mouth, etc., versus leads you pay for.

- **Conversion rate:** The percentage of prospects who become paying customers.

- **Number of support tickets created:** The number of unique issues your support team handles.

- **First support response time:** How long it takes a support person to respond to an inquiry.

- **Time to close support ticket:** How long it takes your support team to solve a customer's problem.

- **Churn:** The annual percentage of customers who stop subscribing to your service.

- **Active users:** Customers using your product.

- **Monthly recurring revenue (MRR):** Your reliable, repeating subscription revenue stream.

- **Total annual recurring revenue (ARR):** Yearly revenue from new sales, renewals, and upgrades adjusted for downgrades and churn.

- **Annual contract value (ACV):** The average annual revenue received from a customer.

- **Lifetime value (LTV):** The predicted total value of a customer over the life of the relationship including the value of upgrades.

What metrics should you be tracking? You may already have a list, but consider this an opportunity to revisit it and make sure that you are watching the performance indicators that are most important to the success of your business. And when you figure out what they are, make sure you can create your own red thread of strategy and link it to everything that you do.

Be grateful

At Aha! we give a lot of ourselves to our customers to help them be their best. We do not charge for consulting or professional services. We humbly and transparently share our experiences and stories. We enjoy it, and that is how we transfer value to the people who make it possible for us to do what we do.

"I was a customer of Aha! before I worked here," said Justin Woods, who is on our Customer Success team.

Building Lovable Products

Put The Responsive Method to work and act now to create more customer value.

Think and feel **(Get inside the pain)**	It starts with empathy — understanding what the customer is thinking and feeling and why. To have empathy for your customers, you need to understand their lives. Learn what they care about and what they fear.
First one focus, **second one free**	It is critical to do one thing well and continue to work on it until you do it brilliantly. If you get it right and you build something lovable, you will find opportunities to expand and solve more problems for more customers.
Prioritize **everything**	To create something special, every aspect of the customer experience matters. Everything you work on must be great. But where to start? Start with strategic goals. If something is not strategic, do not work on it.
Differentiate **everywhere**	Use every touch point to let your customers know that your philosophy, business model, people, and culture are unique and worth paying a premium for. For every interaction is a chance to differentiate your business.
Intercept **and engage**	Reimagine how you view sales and support. Are you offering support willingly and enthusiastically? Create human interactions — intercept customers at the moment of their greatest need and engage them in a meaningful way.
Ship, ship, ship	Have a clear plan and keep shipping. It accelerates value creation and reduces risk. You know where you are going. Any time you can do something small with your product that is aligned with your vision and creates delight, do it.
Stop to smash bugs	When you find a problem, drop everything. Discover the nature of the bug and fix it. This circles back to being interrupt-driven. If bugs are not squashed immediately, they linger, multiply, and grow.
Get real	A company does not do anything. People do. If you want customers to love your product, be authentic. Authenticity is relevant everywhere and every day. It starts with being confident about why you are in business in the first place.
Give, give, give	You do not need to go to extremes to create customer delight. But maybe you should. What are some outrageous ways to make life better for customers? They do not all have to be dramatic; small things make a big difference too.
Report on progress	In order to achieve your goals you need to put metrics in place to evaluate your progress towards them. You cannot improve what you cannot measure. It will keep you accountable to your objectives and motivated to reach them.

Justin goes on to explain:

I led a digital team at Vodafone in the U.K. and I was looking for a product that would bring my team and the entire department together. I found Aha! and fell in love with the product and the company. So I've been on both sides. As a customer, the interrupt-driven side of things makes you feel important. It feels like there is someone on the end of the email or phone just for you. When you need answers, you get them. I've worked for public sector companies where things take weeks or months to do, and when you say, "Can I have this information?" and someone comes back in an hour, you're not expecting that. It can't help but evoke an emotional response in people, and that's why they get so behind TRM.

When I started looking for a new job, I had already resigned from Vodafone without having anywhere else to go. I said, "I need to do the next job for me. I need to go somewhere and do something that makes me happy." I wanted to do something where I could help people like me find the Aha! tool like I did and help them make things better. I've worked for big corporations in my time — IBM, Dell, Vodafone — and I wanted to work on building something that was smaller, more agile, and took roadblocks away. I wanted to be closer to the customer and make a difference. I found that at Aha! the frictionless way we do business disarms customers — they don't know what to do with it. But they love it. And I love being part of the team.

TRM is a movement. Gradually, we are changing how other companies build products. We are changing how they innovate. That's powerful. When we say, "We help product managers build products that people love and be happy doing it," we are confident that we are accomplishing that, because customers keep telling us it's true.

You are what you build. We are fortunate to be able to amplify our impact on the world through TRM and the incredible work that our customers do. We want the world to be a better place, one product at a time.

WORDS TO LOVE BY

- **Software is a service business**
  Because today's customer rents software, success hinges less on features and functionality and more on the experience that employees provide to your customers through personal attention, listening, learning about their needs, solving problems, and helping them accomplish meaningful things with your tools.

- **You are what you build**
  The values and sense of purpose in your organization will shape the products you build and determine the nature and quality of your Complete Product Experience (CPE). Especially in software, products end up being a reflection of people and their leadership.

- **Court "success disasters"**
  These occur when you have sufficient confidence in your team and their abilities to adopt a "we'll take care of that problem if it happens" attitude in your business. If the problem of how to quickly scale does arise, the responsiveness and purpose of The Responsive Method (TRM) can turn it into an opportunity to innovate, discover, or show your commitment to customers. That is a success disaster.

- **TRM is a relevance framework**
  It not only keeps your organization responsive, transparent, and communicative, but it also ensures that what you are learning about your customers — and what you are giving them in response to their needs — is relevant to their goals and challenges at the time. This also keeps your activity relevant to your organization's goals.

- **Use TRM as a guide to your work and building a CPE:**

Think and feel

The first rule of TRM in building product is simple: Approach customers with empathy. Hire people who can understand customer situations and challenges and understand what is meaningful to them. When people can get inside your customers' heads and hearts, they can deliver delight.

First one focus, second one free

Young companies are often tempted to add products or initiatives and "be all things to all people" in the belief that this enhances their chances of survival. But the opposite is true: It pulls their focus away from what they do best. Stay focused on your core product until you do it brilliantly. If you do, other opportunities will present themselves and you will be able to choose the ones you pursue according to your goals and values.

Prioritize everything

All aspects of a product are important, but strategy determines what gets your company's attention and resources at a given time. The "red thread of strategy" should run through all your initiatives as a guide. What are your goals? What problems are you trying to solve? Who are your customers and what do they need? Let strategy dictate every choice your product development teams make.

Differentiate everywhere

Many technologies are being commoditized and consumers are more willing than ever to abandon one provider for another. The key factor is not features but service. People are loyal to businesses that take care of them and appreciate them. Use every touch point with your customers to show that you are paying attention, that you care, and that you are dedicated to solving their problems. If you do, you can rethink how you sell and support customers and change the types of people that you hire for those roles.

Intercept and engage

Too many companies actively avoid human contact, seeing it as a cost rather than a strategic asset. Instead, go out of your way to initiate one-to-one communication with customers. Use technology to intercept their questions and reach out. You'll surprise and delight them and create countless windows to learn more about what they want and how you can become their solution.

Ship, ship, ship

Send useful updates and features often, even if you are only giving customers something small. People love that "getting something in the mail" anticipation and it actually reduces the risk of releasing bad product.

Stop to smash bugs

Drop everything when a problem with your product does arise. Nothing else matters when someone reports a bug. Customers will base a great deal of their view of your company on how well you respond to trouble. Smashing bugs immediately will also help you avoid being buried by technical debt.

Get real

Your company is made of people; everything else is policy and legal procedure. Invest in employees and trust them to solve problems. Have a purpose for every communication with a customer. Be clear, transparent, free of hierarchies, and human.

Give, give, give

Go out of your way to do small or unexpected things that will delight your customers and remind them that you are people, too. These generous gestures need not be as dramatic as sending a steak to Newark Airport to a hungry traveler, but they should be sincere and intended to make customers' lives better, nothing more.

Report on progress against measurable goals
Continually check your company's progress against a set of empirical metrics for growth, revenue, and performance.

- **Be grateful**
Remember that you are here to serve and that it is an honor to have your customer's business. People are why you are in business, and they are your business.

Chapter Nine

BEING A LOVABLE COMPANY

Lovability is a virtuous cycle. Sometimes it's company first and then product and other times it's reversed. That became obvious as I started thinking about writing this book. One does not necessarily need to come before the other, but they both need to be present for love from customers and employees to last.

Consider Toms, the socially conscious shoe and accessory company we talked about in chapter 4. The company was founded by Blake Mycoskie, who calls himself Chief Shoe Giver in a nod to their "One for One" business model. For every product purchased, the company sends a similar product to a person in need. Toms also empowers employees to have a positive impact on the world. They develop original ideas for socially responsible small businesses in their free time, and every month the company provides up to $10,000 in grant funds to start one of those projects.[1]

The company has become a movement of its own, sponsoring events like One Day Without Shoes and World Sight Day to raise awareness about poverty and preventable visual impairment, and the Toms Social Entrepreneurship Fund invests in next-generation social entrepreneurs.

Admirable as it is, this activity would not mean as much if Toms was not a successful business. However, it is, with an estimated $392 million in revenue last year and a valuation of about $625 million.[2] The company has a "customers for life" strategy that focuses on relationships and community, and hundreds of Toms Campus Clubs regularly participate in company events and send messages of affection back to the company. In other words, Toms is beloved.

There are many ways to earn the love of employees. Hamdi Ulukaya, founder of multi-billion dollar yogurt maker Chobani, made headlines when he awarded his two thousand full-time employees stock worth up to 10 percent of the company's value when it goes public or is sold. Ulukaya said in a letter to staff, "This isn't a gift. It's a mutual promise to work together with a shared purpose and responsibility. To continue to create something special and of lasting value."[3]

Apart from making instant global news, the stock award was also a shrewd business move. Research from The University of Pennsylvania shows that employee-owned companies — even ones in which employees are minority owners — outperform their competitors.[4] It is true that Ulukaya now has a slightly smaller stake in Chobani. But it is likely worth a lot more, especially when you consider this research and how employee owners are incentivized to work harder toward the success of the business.

Love Does Not Equal Warm and Fuzzy

The Chobani example in particular shows that a lovable company need not be a warm, fuzzy place where making everyone happy is more important than meaningful goals or profit. The award was given after the company was already a major success.

Relationships with lovable companies tend to make customers express strong emotions, but that does not make those emotions the companies' objectives. They are a by-product of a lovable Complete Product Experience (CPE). Companies that create a lovable CPE do so because they have the DNA to create space for happy employees and internal lovability.

Amazon is a terrific example, though if you read *The New York Times* exposé that ran on August 15, 2015, you may wonder how that is possible. The story portrayed Amazon as a ruthless, punishing workplace where employees are pushed beyond their limits and encouraged to undermine one another — where, according to numerous reports, people facing life challenges ranging from miscarriages to cancer were treated with brutal callousness. There is little doubt that in the feature, Amazon management came across as heartless and cruel. But are they?

Reading interviews with current and former Amazon employees, it is apparent that they love the company and its culture for driving them to be their best and realize their potential. Fit is an important component of internal lovability, and Amazon seeks it. Informed people who apply there know to expect a demanding, high-pressure experience — and more to the point, the ones who excel *desire* it. Amazon also has some of the highest customer satisfaction ratings among Internet brands, due in great part to the company's demanding, customer-centric culture.

It is also important to acknowledge that the ugliness that was reported to be playing out at Amazon may have been taking place in silos within the company. The employees who left may have been from different internal ecosystems or had different motivations than the employees who stayed. That was my takeaway from CEO Jeff Bezos's response to *The New York Times* article, in which he said, "The article doesn't describe the Amazon I know or the caring Amazonians I work with every day."[5] The controversy is a reminder that The Responsive Method (TRM) values can become diluted at scale or when a company fragments into silos. Lovability takes not only vigilance but care to build TRM into the fabric of the entire organization.

The lesson: There is no one way to be internally lovable. It is always a work in progress.

Building Your Tribe

Many product leaders and marketers that I speak with today promote the idea that your customers' early impressions help build a tribe of loyal advocates.

I like the concept of the tribe. However, it starts long before you make an impression on customers. It all begins with the people who are building the CPE with you. Your team is your core tribe. Lovability begins with a tribe of people who are personally invested in delivering a lovable CPE and care about responding to inquiries, solving problems, getting to know customers, and growing relationships. It takes root when a company operates with integrity and follows a vision that is meaningful to everyone. It grows when leaders share the company's goals with employees while giving them the freedom to achieve their own goals, too. It thrives when owners and executives set clear expectations, express gratitude, and recognize people for their achievements.

Every interaction with employees either reinforces or contradicts your stated values and impacts whether people trust you to do what you say you will do. The stronger that trust, the more likely people are to invest themselves in your business and give everything they have to make it a success.

We have worked hard at Aha! to live up to our promise that we will help employees grow and enjoy better lives. Ask a random sampling of employees, and most will say that they have grown more since joining Aha! than in all of their previous jobs combined. That is not because the job is easy. TRM is demanding. Expectations and rewards are high. The work is intense.

We do not rely on luck for success. No successful business does. We rely on the same resource as any successful company: people who work exceptionally hard, put the team first, and are focused on results.

We do not get that level of performance because of compensation, benefits, and perks. Those are factors, because everyone wants to be well paid and to feel valued. However, I believe that most people want to excel at what they do, and the best people in any field go where they can be great. We give employees an environment in which the only limits to their growth are talent, effort, and an insatiable desire to keep learning. Instead of us saying in a job interview, "This is what we expect of you," our applicants tend to say things like, "These are my expectations for myself and I believe Aha! can help me reach them."

We are enthusiastic about helping employees grow, and that enthusiasm sends a powerful message: We want to see our people spread their wings, even if they do so somewhere else. Does your company send that message? Do you honor employee expectations? Do you have their backs and keep your promises? Your answer will determine the kind of people you hire. Remember, technology changes. Values do not.

The Blueprint for a Lovable Company

Every organization is different, but there are 11 fundamental internal building blocks of lovability that are relevant to the culture of any organization. For companies that practice TRM, these are foundational and naturally complement how they think about customers.

Consider the following a blueprint for improving your company's internal lovability — which will, if followed faithfully, improve the lovability of your CPE as well.

1. Be clear about your purpose

Why are you all working together, doing what you are doing each day? In a successful company, every employee is a leader, so everyone should know the answer to this question.

The purpose of business is to build a profitable company. You accomplish that by serving customers and creating real value. The meaning of value will be different for each organization, but you must know what value looks like for you and the people who do the work. Know what kind of company you want to be and what kind of value you want to deliver.

If you are the CEO, you must continually provide clarity and focus around your purpose and the big, strategic initiatives that serve that purpose. You define what success means and guide people back to purpose if they wind up in the weeds. I do this by sharing strategic goals and initiatives with every employee through the Aha! application and reporting on our progress every week at an all-company meeting.

Great leaders also support and motivate people to go after success aggressively and passionately. You are their safety net, reminding them that if they stumble, you and the team leaders in the company will pick them up, dust them off, and get them moving again. No one should fear failure in a TRM organization.

2. Value work

It is a very human trait to love achievement and want the opportunity to do something important. Everything about your company — from its vision to how people collaborate — should send the message that doing great work is valuable unto itself and will also bring acknowledgement and material rewards.

TRM organizations are intrinsically motivated. They eagerly point out that work has value in and of itself. That is why no one at Aha! is compensated through commissions. Commission-based systems motivate the wrong behavior. Compensation is important, but pay and benefits should be where the rewards of work begin, not where they end.

We all are partially motivated by self-interest and our desire to live well, so every company must compensate people well enough so they can live comfortably. But being productive and making a meaningful difference in other people's lives is the higher reward of work. It gets people engaged and caring about what they do. Be sure your organization is promoting that idea as a core principle and recognizing those who embody the love of doing good work for its own sake.

3. Reject work/life balance

Work is part of life, not separate from it. We spend 40 to 80 hours a week on the job. We should aspire to have our work be as satisfying and fulfilling as all the other parts of our lives. Lovable companies focus on sustainable happiness at work and away from it.

I have a number of passions — family, work, cycling, backpacking, travel, and photography are some of them. I look for ways to find sustainable happiness in everything I do. In fact, I worked on chapters of this book while in Scotland, where I enjoyed a holiday break with my wife and our three boys.

I shared photos of the Scottish isles and countryside with the Aha! team along the way. And I shared what I was working on with my family. It is important to me that my boys see how passionate I am about my work and how much effort it takes to build something great.

The best companies award and fuel hard work, in part with a culture of autonomy and growth. They reject the concept that employees can find work/ life balance and help them time-slice their days to get the most out of them, no matter what they are working on. They trust employees to solve problems, self-motivate, and be accountable — and they find that they are happy to do it. They understand that work should renew and revive, not exhaust.

Challenging environments give people audacious goals and the room to stretch and reach them. They demand from employees more than they thought they could deliver and then give them space to deliver their best. They stimulate creative thinking, which results in better products, happier customers, and committed teams. They lead to a better life.

> "Challenging environments give people audacious goals and the room to stretch and reach them."

4. 100 + 100 = 100

This might seem strange if you have always given more than you received from your employers. In many larger companies, the employer is the center of power. People join the company, collect a paycheck, and work. The employee puts in 70 percent of the effort and the employer gives 30 percent back. That is a recipe for cynicism, resentment, and turnover.

In a TRM company, the employer and employee are equally responsible for each other's well-being and give everything they have to support each other. Some time ago, one of our employees needed to rush her daughter to the emergency room. Her colleague picked up her scheduled customer demo with about three minutes' notice, no questions asked. Why wouldn't he? He was available and she needed someone to help. And you already learned that we encouraged two employees to step away from the company to work on non-Aha! projects that were important to them.

This mindset encourages everyone to put the good of the team first. That breeds deep, mutual trust. Think of it like a marriage. Both partners may believe that they are giving 100 percent to the relationship, but if one is falling short, trust breaks down. Resentment and an "every man for himself" mentality takes over.

Most organizations do not operate like this, so employees are often skeptical. Even people who start working at Aha! and learn how we operate do not always believe it. That is why, while the employer-employee relationship is a two-way street, the employer must set the example. Unconditional support must start with company leaders. When employees see the company acting on the 100 + 100 = 100 principle, they will reciprocate.

5. Be anywhere

According to a 2016 FlexJobs survey, 81 percent of respondents also say they would be more loyal to their employers if they had flexible work options.[6] That is a missed opportunity. Many businesses would benefit from letting employees work from where they are happy. Executives might fret about motivation and control, but there is a solution: Hire intrinsically motivated people, give them clear goals, and offer them the tools to be successful. As long as they meet their objectives, provide an outstanding CPE, and are happy doing both, it should not matter where or even when they get the work done.

Aha! has never had an office of any size. Employees on three continents continue to work from home or other locations of their own choosing. While that has helped us grow by reducing our overhead, remote work also gives us access to a larger, deeper pool of talent. We aspire to make employees' lives better, and inviting them to work with Aha! without asking them to relocate is powerful proof of our sincerity. Remote work means we do not disqualify skilled, values-driven people based on geography.

Consider that people are not just trying to be great for you. They are also working at being great for their family, friends, and communities. Help them achieve that goal and their gratitude and commitment will help your business thrive.

"Since joining Aha! I've had 150-plus mornings sipping coffee with my girls as the school bus arrives — more than I had in my entire career beforehand," said Donna Sawyer, who I first introduced you to in chapter 1. "Could I run a large portfolio of products and travel to conferences and customers all the time? Sure. But that's not what I want. There are more of me out there, too — people looking for a way to work that also lets them enjoy their families and friends and be engaged in their communities."

Being open to letting people work where they want could greatly expand your potential talent pool, as it has for us. There is also strong evidence that remote work reduces employee stress, improves health, and increases productivity — not to mention reducing vehicle emissions because people are not commuting to an office.

6. Teach hard

Giving people goals stretches them and brings them to life, so we never stop teaching. After they accept a role with us, we ask every employee to read a changing roster of three books. Right now, they are *Mindset: The New Psychology of Success* by Carol Dweck; *How Will You Measure Your Life?* by Clayton Christensen, James Allworth, and Karen Dillon; and *Drive: The Surprising Truth About What Motivates Us* by Daniel Pink. The books are important but so is the message they send: Aha! is a learning organization. Everyone is constantly learning, exploring, and discovering. You are expected to be a student and we will pay you to keep learning.

We also assign a book on a key theme twice a year. When we get together for our weeklong, all-company, on-site meetings, each member of the team is responsible for a short presentation about the book. The book is always about personal growth, not the business.

As I have already mentioned, everyone goes through a four-week onboarding training program during which they become an honorary Customer Success person. After that, they provide live support to real customers and, in the process, learn about TRM. When they run one of our many live customer demos, they graduate. People hired to work in Customer Success go through an even more intense eight-week program to make sure they are ready to deliver the delightful CPE that we are known for.

We also give direct feedback — especially to those who work with customers — and maintain internal coaching programs that help people improve their skills. We hire experts in product and technology and then teach them hard about all the other things they need to do to discover what customers are interested in, help them find value, and build relationships over the long term.

7. Grow your talent

Promote from within. Build a framework, train people on it, give them the room to grow, then take advantage of that growth. Hire well, build a deep bench, and trust that people will step up when you need them to.

That is the advantage to hiring experts and investing in their continued learning. When opportunities come up to step into leadership roles, they are up to the challenge. It also reflects our commitment to bringing on professionals who crave achievement. Rather than shy away from a challenge and the risk it implies, they lean into it. It helps that the Aha! culture is nurturing and supportive. Employees taking a step up the career ladder know that if they stumble, someone will be there to catch them.

This ensures continuity and smooth transitions, no small consideration when every day means more pivotal customer interactions. For example, when Suzanne Vaughan, our former Senior Director of Customer Success, left to pursue a career as an executive coach, Melissa Hopkins was ready to step right into Suzanne's shoes. We were able to keep serving customers and growing the business like nothing had happened.

8. Honor reality

Many companies are built around the idea that to grow value you must manipulate how people perceive your company. Business becomes about creating the appearance of value instead of creating actual value. One is about pursuing valuation — the other is about creating authentic value.

TRM cannot function in an environment built on spin. Do not invest time or money in manipulating what people think. First, they will know you are manipulating them and resent you for it. Second, as we have seen in the technology sector, managing perceptions leads to unsustainable companies built on hype — companies that do not survive.

Being grounded in reality is a particular challenge at larger companies, where the size of the projects that you lead and the number of people you manage is a sign of your importance. I have been in larger organizations where too many people spent most of their time carefully building their brands and shaping how others perceived them instead of leading. That is a dangerous pattern. When leaders obsess over managing perceptions, others follow. Before you know it, you have an organization that is operating in a parallel universe that no longer reflects reality. It becomes easy to lose sight of the purpose of the business: Building a profitable company by serving customers and creating value.

I am an optimistic realist. I think people can have a positive frame of mind while staying connected to reality. Keep your personal reality as a company leader tied to your vision, but validate it through feedback from customers and colleagues. If your vision and the outside data conflict, have the courage to act on the data.

Most of all, make your organization's reality as compelling as the hype that other companies generate. At Aha! we focus on managing our business, not perceptions. We care deeply about the facts. If you work as hard as you can to achieve your goals, guided by values and purpose, then let the chips fall where they may.

9. Work it

I have suggested in articles prior to writing this book that you can tell if someone will become rich — he or she works harder than everyone else. Whether you measure riches in friendships, fitness, talent, or money, those who have abundance inevitably get it by working harder to secure it. Nothing good was ever accomplished without great effort. The idea that you can work less and build greatness is fool's gold.

For example, you probably know Mark Cuban as an outspoken billionaire, Shark Tank personality, and owner of the NBA's Dallas Mavericks. But long before he was those things, he was co-founder of a system integrator and software reseller called *MicroSolutions*, which he launched in 1983. In 1999 Cuban sold his next company, Broadcast.com, for $5.7 billion, but did you know that he did not take a single vacation day for seven years?[7] During that time, he said he did not even read a book that was not about business or software. There are no overnight successes, but Cuban might be the first "up all night" success.

> "Nothing good was ever accomplished without great effort. The idea that you can work less and build greatness is fool's gold."

There is often a backlash against this sort of single-minded work ethic. People might call you a workaholic or a perfectionist. Some may criticize your inability to set boundaries or worry about burnout. But there is no other way to build a sustainably great business. Putting in the hours makes you a source of new insights and fresh innovations. It sets the example for everyone in your company — *that this is what leads to success*. If you love what you do, the work will not burn you out. It will light you up.

10. Keep pedaling

Running a company, especially a new company still finding its way, is hard work. Refusing to quit when things get hard — being resilient in the face of adversity — is essential. For me, the idea is embodied in Jens Voigt, a famous German cyclist. He would be competing in grueling mountain races when his legs started to burn. When the pain became distracting, he would yell "Shut up, legs!" and continue pedaling.

At some point, all successful people need to block out the pain, yell, "Shut up, legs!" and keep going. Endurance athletes — marathoners, cyclists, triathletes — talk about "out-suffering" the other guy. This is true for companies, too. You need a collection of people who are committed to doing the extra work that other people will not. Find them and reward them and they will make you a huge success.

You have to keep pedaling. When you still have a few miles to go, you have no other option. Eventually, the pain will go away. In business, that means that this, too, shall pass. If things go sideways, tomorrow is a new day. You are going to have to get back to work, turn on the lights, let yesterday go, and keep building toward your goals.

Taking this view may be easier for Aha! because we have created real customer value and are growing quickly. Every day a tranche of new customers signs up. People approach us because they want to work with us. It's a lot easier to "be better tomorrow" when you have a tailwind, because you are delivering a product that solves a real problem and people love working with you.

But that does not mean that we do not have tough days. There was a time when a very talented engineer did not accept our job offer and we had to restart a major project when we figured out that the technical direction we selected was not going to work out. Despite the challenges, we all keep getting better when we remind ourselves of our purpose and focus on serving our customers and colleagues.

Keep learning. Focus. Train harder. Be more transparent. Do one thing that will make customers love you. Then do another. And another, until you radically exceed expectations. That is how you keep pedaling and find your own tailwind.

11. Let go

Sometimes your company will not be a fit for a customer or employee. When that happens, be responsive and level with the person quickly and professionally. Lean on TRM principles of transparency and kindness.

Not being all things to all people is actually a competitive advantage. Remember "first one focus, second one free." If you are appealing to everyone, it means you are not serving anyone particularly well. Not everyone will be a perfect match for you.

Walk away from business that does not fit your goals. We once told a well-known multinational technology company that we no longer wanted to work with them. It was painful, but we had met with them eight times and they still asked for a free six-month product evaluation. The value exchange simply was not there. If business is not a fit, decline it. This will leave you the bandwidth to work with customers who respect your time and effort as much as you respect theirs.

The same is true for prospective employees. Some might have a better opportunity elsewhere, while others are a poor match for the skills you need or your culture. Let them know it is okay for them not to fit. Many people learned during the last recession to behave with desperation, and even though the outlook has brightened, they will press on even if the company's approach makes them miserable. That does not benefit you, them, or our customers. Watch for signs of poor fit and let people move on to what is more likely to bring them sustainable happiness.

The Blueprint for a Lovable Company

Commit to the following playbook to improve your company's internal lovability.

Be clear about your purpose	In a successful company, everyone should know what they are working towards. Define what success means to your business and guide people back to the purpose if they wind up in the weeds.
Value work	It is a human trait to love achievement and the opportunity to do something important. Doing great work is valuable unto itself. It will also bring recognition and material rewards, but effort itself has inherent value.
Reject work/life balance	We should aspire to have our work be as satisfying and fulfilling as all the other parts of our lives. Lovable companies understand that work should renew and revive, not exhaust.
100 + 100 = 100	The company and its employee must both give everything they have — that's the 100 percent. But it starts with company leaders. This mindset encourages everyone to put the good of the team first. That breeds deep, mutual trust.
Be anywhere	Hire intrinsically motivated people, give them clear goals, and offer them the tools to be successful. It should not matter where or even when they get the work done.
Teach hard	Give direct feedback — especially to those who work with customers — and maintain internal coaching programs that help people improve their skills every day. You can never get back today, tomorrow.
Grow your talent	Promote from within. Build a framework for success, train people on it, give them room to grow, then take advantage of that growth. Trust that people will step into challenging roles as the organization needs them to.
Honor reality	Do not invest time or money on manipulation. Work as hard as you can, guided by values and purpose, then let the chips fall where they may.
Work it	Nothing good was ever accomplished without great effort. The idea that you can work less and build greatness is fool's gold. If you love what you do, the work will not burn you out. It will light you up.
Keep pedaling	Refusing to quit when things get hard is essential. Keep learning. Focus. Train harder. Do one thing that will make customers love you. Then do it again and again, until it becomes habit and you have a tailwind at your back.
Let go	Not every customer or employee will be a perfect match for your company. Watch for signs of poor fit and let people move on to what is more likely to bring them sustainable happiness.

Healing

Miserable people build miserable products and miserable companies. You might be miserable at your current job or running your current business. I have been there. Even if you are not miserable, you may have become numb and apathetic. That is even worse because apathetic people do not care what they build or who they serve.

The good news is that a company constructed with TRM building blocks should *heal* its people. Commerce does not have to be a ruthless, brutal enterprise that damages people's lives. It can be a source of happiness, healing, and hope.

When you come into contact with that kind of business, you feel it. When you walk out of a store or hang up after a support call saying, "Wow, that was sure a terrific experience!" you can be certain that the employee you just dealt with is having a terrific work experience. People who feel respected, appreciated, and trusted will always build better products, give better service, and deliver a better CPE.

> "Commerce does not have to be a ruthless, brutal enterprise that damages people's lives. It can be a source of happiness, healing, and hope."

Every company has a purpose: Acquire customers and build a profitable business by serving the customer and creating value. That mission has defined Aha! since the beginning. We asked, "How can we give people something deeply meaningful?" Our answer was to create what was deeply meaningful to *us*. We built a business that treats people the way we always wanted to be treated and crossed our fingers that others would find that as appealing as we did. Fortunately, they have.

Do what makes you happy and heals you and others will be drawn to your vision. Great artists or writers do not produce great work by tailoring it to what they think people will like. They create what speaks to them and if that vision is authentic, other people find their own meaning in it.

TRM Is Work

Building a company around TRM may sound idyllic, but it is not. It is a *lot* of work. The "R" does stand for "responsive," after all. This is an evenings and weekends enterprise. We are always on. Creating a movement is a journey, and like any journey, there is no escalator to get there. We work hard to propel ourselves forward based on a deep sense of purpose and engagement.

Those qualities play into Frederick Herzberg's "two-factor theory." It says that there are two factors that contribute to workplace satisfaction or dissatisfaction. *Hygiene factors* like pay, benefits, vacation time, and advancement opportunities are important, but they do not make people more engaged. *Motivators* like recognition, autonomy, and the chance to do meaningful work do get people engaged and invested in what they do. TRM and lovability work their magic in the motivational space.

If you adopt TRM, you will be asking people to work harder than ever before. You are either all-in or all-out. There can be no halfway. An anecdote from Jamey Iaccino, from our People Success team, illustrates this. "I was speaking with a candidate who was passionate about a company he had founded and still ran," Jamey said. "I told him we were looking for somebody who could be dedicated to just Aha! for this position, and he spent the next few minutes trying to convince me that he was such a good manager that he could easily do multiple jobs. I told him that if he really loved his other business that much, he should go do that and be happy."

> "Creating a movement is a journey, and like any journey, there is no escalator to get there."

Lovability requires a 24/7 focus on product and human interaction — there is no break. Because of this, people will not dedicate themselves to the demands of TRM because of hygiene factors like pay and benefits. They have to love what they do and why they do it. You have to love people and want the best for them. If that love exists on both sides, customers will engage because you make them feel like contributors to something genuine and meaningful.

Employees will be committed because it will give them the greatest space they have ever had to build something meaningful and lasting.

You will be vulnerable

Building lovability also means accepting a level of fear and vulnerability. Openness and transparency means you will take it on the chin once in a while. But that is a risk that is well worth the possible return. There is value in the journey — employees will not be the only ones becoming better people.

Intentions matter. If you give an initiative your full effort and fail, most people will appreciate and applaud you for what you did accomplish and forgive what you did not. Plan with the information you have and act.

Remember that you will never control everything about your business. You might invest considerable time and effort into a customer only to find that their business is struggling and they no longer have the budget to purchase from you. You might invest in developing a promising employee into a star only to have him decide that he wants to go back to school for an advanced degree. It happens. Being lovable means being vulnerable. The only alternative is not to be lovable, and that is no alternative at all.

TRM gives you exactly what you put into it.

Go get busy

As I have said, TRM is really a movement. It helps entrepreneurs build what Lars Dalgaard, founder and former CEO of SuccessFactors, calls "weatherproof companies." In writing about the concept — and explaining why he was able to sell SuccessFactors for 11 times revenues back in 2012 — he said that he built SuccessFactors for the long haul and tough weather, referencing football teams who can clench wins in tough weather like the Green Bay Packers. The focus was on values and good people who got plenty of coaching and support. They invited constant feedback, built a values-driven culture around gratitude and respect, and paid attention to reality, not spin.[8]

When the company was acquired for $3.4 billion, it was the right decision for everyone. The management team and owners were prepared to *not* sell and to keep running the company if they did not like the fit with the buyer.[9]

Lovability works. TRM and relationship building work. Entrepreneurs and business leaders are beginning to figure that out. One early indicator is data showing that the number of U.S.-based call center jobs is actually *increasing* because companies that serve customers here realize that better customer support is critical to customer satisfaction and profitability.[10] They are starting to understand what our grandparents understood: People will always choose to work with someone who makes them feel heard, respected, and understood. And they will love people who respond to them instantly. That is as true in technology as in any other business.

Melissa Hopkins, who also creates training videos for us, ends each one with: "Go get busy." That has become a catchphrase that our customers repeat back to us, and I would like to close this part of the book with it.

I have shown you the path and franchised what success looks like. Now, go get busy. Use your talents to pursue success and happiness on your terms. Go and be your best. If you stumble, that is all right. When you need help, we will be here, as responsive as ever.

WORDS TO LOVE BY

- **Lovable products come from lovable companies**

  Building a business of people who feel part of something meaningful and love what they do will lead to a lovable Complete Product Experience.

- **Lovability does not mean warm and fuzzy**

  Amazon built a company that people love but is also a challenging place to work. Setting clear expectations and rewarding those who can meet them is critical.

- **Give people an environment to grow**

  One where they can aspire to whatever levels of achievement their talent and work ethic will allow. Human beings relish the chance to achieve.

- **Know your purpose**

  Define the organization's vision and values for everyone and adhere to them, especially in your actions as leader.

- **Trust doing good work**

  It has intrinsic value and is its own reward.

- **Reject work/life balance**

  Work should add quality to life and be as satisfying and fulfilling as family time and leisure time.

- **100 + 100 = 100**

  Employer and employee should be prepared to give everything they have and have each other's back. However, the employer is responsible for creating an environment where employees feel safe doing that.

- **Be everywhere**
  You expand your talent pool if people can stay where they are happy.

- **Teach hard**
  Training and learning should be part of your company's DNA. Give people goals, stretch them, and challenge them to grow.

- **Grow your talent**
  Promote from within and build a deep bench. Just know that you will lose some great people after investing in them.

- **Love reality and hate perception management**
  People should be less concerned about managing how they are seen in the company and more concerned with creating a reality that exceeds the promise of other companies' hype.

- **Work it**
  There is no substitute for big effort. People and companies that work harder are rewarded proportionally for their work and get better faster than others do.

- **Keep pedaling**
  When things go sideways, get back up and keep pedaling. The successful entrepreneur is often the one who doesn't stay down.

- **Let it go**

  Do not be all things to all people. Do not be afraid to walk away from business that is a bad fit, or to let employees go do something that will make them happier.

- **A lovable business is a healing business**

  Your business should do meaningful things that make everyone feel part of something worthwhile and important. Miserable people build miserable products.

- **The Responsive Method and lovability take effort**

  They are 24/7, all-in propositions. You cannot half-commit and expect to have success. Anyone who cannot invest fully should work somewhere else.

- **Lovability means risking much and sometimes, you will lose**

  But building a weatherproof company that can keep going in tough times and enjoy success over the long term means accepting those losses — because they will be more than balanced by the gains.

♡ *Chapter Ten*

THE LOVABILITY TOOLKIT

You now know the power of lovability to win customers and drive sustainable growth. But how do you know if you are on track? Using the tools in this chapter, you can assess how lovable your products and company are today and discover what you can expect when you achieve true lovability.

The important thing to remember is that a lovable Complete Product Experience (CPE) benefits everyone. Customers benefit by gaining mojo, that feeling of confidence and potency they get when they use a product that expands their capacity. They feel more competent and able to deliver meaningful results, and they might even enjoy financial and career rewards because your company's lovable CPE makes them better at their job. Do that and you will earn loyal customers for life who work with you to guarantee your success.

I call that *allegiance*, and that is what lovability will bring your company. Allegiance is that state in which the customer feels that you are both on the same side and will expend personal and political capital to go to bat for your company by giving referrals, defending you against detractors, and expanding their relationship with you.

A great example is Chipotle Mexican Grill, which has always been extremely responsive to customer concerns about issues like genetically modified food and local sourcing. When the company was caught in a storm of negative publicity in 2015 over an outbreak of food-borne illness at many of its restaurants, that allegiance paid off. Customers fought hard for Chipotle, something unheard of for a company that is the fastest-growing in its sector. So while the company's net income fell 44 percent in the fourth quarter of 2015, fans of its local, sustainable cuisine helped it remain solidly profitable. Progress towards regaining customer trust has been steady. In fact, the company announced plans to open roughly 200 new restaurants in 2017.[1]

For the company owner and investor, lovability leads to profitability and the creation of long-term value. Research into *customer delight* (the closest analog to love I could find in academic literature) shows that while delighted customers put an organization in the position of having to meet increased expectations, delight also increases profitability and gives organizations a significant competitive advantage.

Companies that foster delight/love can maintain higher margins because their customers are willing to pay a premium for a wonderful experience. They often enjoy lower costs because they have happier employees who are intrinsically motivated to complete projects on time and deliver quality. Finally, they grow organically — and often rapidly — through referrals from an unpaid but passionate sales force: customers who love the product and the business.

At Aha! we have seen a "pay it forward" benefit because of our focus on lovability. People who use our product can build more lovable products themselves, and in turn they can make life better for *their* customers. Software is about improving work and how we experience life. If we improve how another organization works, that will have a positive impact on their customers and employees. That is what I mean when I say that lovability and The Responsive Method (TRM) is a movement. We hope to change the way people do business and enhance the quality of their lives.

Do you want in on all this love, growth, and allegiance? Do not delay. Start your own assessment and find out how to grow your lovability. We have provided tools to help you assess the lovability of both your products and your company.

Part One: Lovable Product Assessment

These surveys will tell you how customers feel about your CPE. The first two are to be used internally and are more comprehensive. They should be used quarterly in most organizations so you can compare the results over time. Because they are internally generated benchmarks, they should be completed anonymously.

The third is a compelling way to get a quick read directly from your customers. I suggest making it a part of your feedback process and reporting on it monthly to understand how your lovability is changing.

Lovability Building Blocks

To be completed by your internal teams, including senior executives, product directors, product managers, and directors of customer success. For an explanation of each metric, please refer back to chapter 3. Rank the presence of each Building Block on a 1–5 scale:

5 = Customers always express this about our product.
4 = Customers regularly express this about our product.
3 = Customers sometimes express this about our product.
2 = Customers express this about our product rarely.
1 = Customers express this about our product once every other year.

Hope	5	4	3	2	1
Satisfaction	5	4	3	2	1
Care	5	4	3	2	1
Confidence	5	4	3	2	1
Trust	5	4	3	2	1
Scale	5	4	3	2	1
Sustainability	5	4	3	2	1
Motivation	5	4	3	2	1
Fun	5	4	3	2	1
Halo	5	4	3	2	1

Add all 10 ratings for your Lovability Building Blocks score: _____

Lovability Signs

To be completed by your internal teams, including marketers, salespeople, customer success, and professional services.

For an explanation of each sign, please refer back to chapter 3. Rank the presence of each Lovability Sign on a 1–3 scale:

3 = Customers regularly do this.
2 = Customers sometimes do this.
1 = Customers rarely do this.

Hugs	3	2	1
Love Notes	3	2	1
Megaphones	3	2	1

Add all three ratings for your Lovability Signs score: _____

Add together the Lovability Building Blocks and Lovability Signs scores.

Total score: _____

Interpreting your score

50–59 **High lovability**

You are a trusted friend. You have enthusiastic customers who express love for you and your company regularly, and contribute to your long-term success.

40–49 **Medium lovability**

You are reliable but not inspiring. You have some passionate customers but would like more expressions of love and deeper relationships. Work on things like responsiveness, authenticity, and empathy.

30–39 **Low lovability**

You deliver a few sparks of joy. You have your moments, but customers are more apathetic than enthusiastic and you are hard-selling them more than they are buying. There is a lot of work to do, starting with questioning your company's values, purpose, and relationship with customers.

<30   **No lovability**

Your customers are indifferent or actually dislike your company. Radical intervention is called for if you hope to survive (especially if you are not a monopoly). The only place to go from here is up, so stay strong.

Customer Lovability

To be completed by all customers.

The Customer Lovability survey is designed to reveal opinions about your CPE, which includes the core offering and all of the services and customer touch points that surround it. While the two previous lovability surveys measure internal perceptions, your Customer Lovability score measures external customer opinions, so it has the strongest implications for your true market lovability.

Ask customers to complete this assessment online or embed it into your product surveys and/or communications on a regular basis. Report on the changes monthly, quarterly, or following a new product launch or change in how you interact with customers.

Here is an example of the messaging you can use when you roll the survey out to your customers:

Please rate your Complete Product Experience with [product name]. Please consider the quality and performance of our product and your interactions with our team on a 1–10 scale.

Customer Lovability

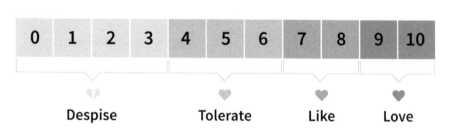

Customer Lovability score = average customer rating

Interpreting your score

The Customer Lovability score equals the average customer rating for any given survey or series of surveys over a determined time frame.

You can also consider interpreting what customers are telling you via the survey as follows:

9–10 **Love**

The complete product experience is exceptional and has earned their loyalty and love.

7–8 **Like**

The complete product experience is consistently good and occasionally delights them.

4–6 **Tolerate**

The complete product experience is mediocre but they grudgingly accept it.

0–3 **Despise**

The complete product experience leaves them feeling unhappy and often resentful.

Do not worry if your Customer Lovability score starts out lower than you might have expected. Remember that the goal is to increase your score over time using the principles in this book.

You could also use the survey to assess specific interactions — for example, the lovability of your customer support calls. Send it to customers following a support interaction and ask, "How much did you love your interaction with us today?"

Part Two: How Lovable Is Your Company?

The Employee Lovability survey is designed to reveal the lovability of your internal culture. Since lovable companies produce lovable products, it is important to check in with employees regularly to find out if your organization is purpose-driven, growing in-house talent, helping the team accomplish meaningful things, and exhibiting the other telltale signs of employee lovability.

Ask employees to complete this confidential survey quarterly so you can assess your progress in building a lovable company.

Employee Lovability

To be completed by all employees.

For an explanation of each metric, please refer back to chapter 9. Rank the presence of each characteristic on a 1–5 scale:

5 = The company embodies this every day; it is in its DNA.
4 = The company demonstrates this most of the time, but not always.
3 = The company demonstrates this inconsistently but has good intentions.
2 = The company talks about this but does not back it up with much action.
1 = The company could not care less about this.

Have purpose	5	4	3	2	1
Value work	5	4	3	2	1
Reject work/life	5	4	3	2	1
100 + 100 = 100	5	4	3	2	1
Be anywhere	5	4	3	2	1
Teach hard	5	4	3	2	1
Grow talent	5	4	3	2	1
Honor reality	5	4	3	2	1
Work it	5	4	3	2	1
Keep pedaling	5	4	3	2	1
Let go	5	4	3	2	1

Add all 11 ratings for your Employee Lovability score: _____

Interpreting your score

50–55 Extreme lovability

You have built a sustainably happy organization where people are engaged in meaningful work and feel respected. You are experiencing high degrees of customer love and employee loyalty.

44–49 High lovability

Your culture is strong, and while you have not reached that "championship team" feeling yet, you are on your way.

38–43 Moderate lovability

There is some loyalty and feeling of mission among your employees, but something is missing. Do you have clearly stated values that are fairly steady? Do people act according to them? Have you helped your team grow? Given them autonomy and trust?

32–37 Low lovability

Turnover is a problem, trust and engagement are low, and it will take a serious refocus on transparency, accountability, and employee happiness to turn things around.

<32 No lovability

Your people are working for the paycheck and living in fear of being fired (or desperately searching for a new job). No one loves your company. You need to reinvent your entire culture.

Lovability Is an Adventure

Lovability is one of the most noble adventures you will pursue. If you are fortunate, it will become your life's work. And every adventure that is worth pursuing has its unexpected twists and turns. That is why you need to know what signposts to look for to identify whether you are on the right path.

We hope that you are ready for your own exciting journey and that we have given you a meaningful map to follow and tools that can help you and your team build lovable products and organizations.

I would love to know what happens when you start to incorporate the principles of lovability and The Responsive Method into your personal and business go-forward actions. Send me postcards along the way @bdehaaff or brian.dehaaff@aha.io and I hope that our paths lead us to a meaningful intersection.

ACKNOWLEDGMENTS

I wrote a thesis my last semester before graduating from the greatest university in the world, The University of California at Berkeley. It was lousy.

OK, that assessment might be a bit too tough. The thesis was satisfactory but not great. I ran out of steam to do what was necessary to make it an exceptional work. And as someone who aims for perfection, I was not proud of it. I vowed never to publish any type of long-form content again.

So, what happened? How did I go from there to publishing my first book? Hard work, good fortune, and great tragedy. That's what happened.

I was fortunate to build and sell two traditionally funded software companies to well-known public companies within a few years. That experience gave me and my co-founder, Dr. Chris Waters, the confidence to start a new company and craft it in a nontraditional way for a Silicon Valley-based software company. We wanted to build a company that was completely aligned with our own values and remain in control of its future. That company was Aha!

And it worked remarkably well. But in 2013, as Aha! emerged as the obvious choice for companies looking to improve how they innovated and built products, my family was struggling with an all-too-common sadness. My sister-in-law, Sarah Haberfeld de Haaff, had become very ill and later died from complications of breast cancer on February 23, 2015. She was only 40.

Sarah was someone everyone wanted to know. She led with her heart and taught those who had no voice how to speak. Sarah's last lesson was one of hope, through her embrace of the contradictions in life that we all live with. She opened her soul even when she was suffering and invited the entire community to see what it meant to face incurable illness with courage and dignity.

And she wrote. Her writings during her illness were numerous. She told stories with the wit of a comic and the grit of a boxer. She became known for her love of the ampersand because it gave her the symbol she needed to explain to the rest of us how she could be both happy & sad and hopeful & petrified and sick & well — all at the same time.

I am indebted to Sarah for reminding me that everything we do is personal and that writing is one way we can move forward. You can actually be supposed opposites at the same time. For example, in my world, there is no split between my business self and personal self or work and life. There is just life, and only action can help us remember and forget. And all we can do each day is work to build what we believe in. Everything we do is work, and we are compensated in different ways, depending on what we are working on and for.

I believe deeply in every person's potential to work and create meaningful value. I believe in human-centered business to help each of us realize our best. And I am committed to helping others build lovable products and businesses through relentless effort, an allergy to boredom, and no drama. I am convinced that The Responsive Method is the best way to do so.

But The Responsive Method was only a fledgling idea when Chris and I started Aha!, and I am indebted to him for helping make those early notions a reality. Without his technical genius, unrelenting work ethic, and desire to make everything we do at Aha! great, this book would never exist. He is also a quiet and thoughtful friend who is always up for adventure.

Two founders hardly make a meaningful company, though. That is why employees are the most important component of any organization. Aha! comprises the greatest collection of talented, productive, and kind people that I have ever worked with. There is no comparison.

You get a behind-the-curtains view of the world-class team at Aha! throughout this book, and I was flattered that so many people wanted to be interviewed for this project. I thank each one of them, everyone who provided feedback throughout the writing process, and every person on the team. You are making it easier for people to build great products and be happy doing it. Leading Aha! is a privilege, and I am honored and humbled every day by the magnitude of what we accomplish.

I want to share special gratitude to Greenleaf Book Group for choosing to publish this book and to Molly Jane Quinn. Molly leads special marketing projects and our content efforts at Aha! and is a world-class editor and author. While she joined the company after most of the manuscript was drafted, she expertly managed the process to publish the book. She took great pride in the success of the project, as if it were her own, and I only wish we started working together much earlier. Much, much earlier. She would have helped make my college thesis great.

And while employees are the most important people at any company, they will not be working together for long without a meaningful group of committed customers. I have been humbled by the feedback and growth of Aha! and the sheer volume and caliber of customers that we work with. Over 100,000 people depend on Aha! every day, and many of them have shared their love for Aha! and ideas for how we can make it better. Thank you, and please keep it up. We are listening.

I was deeply moved that many of our customers and friends of Aha! were willing to share their experiences and stories with me. Special thanks go to Michel Besner, Serge Doubinski, Charles Du, Joshua Lipp, Shardul Mehta, John Peters, Art Swanson, Suzanne Vaughan, and Paul Zuber.

And finally, this book is for the people who always come first — family. This project and my life are truly grandpa-inspired. My parents, my brother and me, and our kids are what our grandparents struggled for and their parents fled heinous oppression to make possible. My achievement is centuries in the making and the result of our ancestors' dedication to learning and my parents' emphasis on education. I come from a lineage of people who had an

NOTES

Part I: Grandpa-Inspired

INTRODUCTION

1. Dave Michaels and Telis Demos, "SEC's White Warns Silicon Valley on Valuations," *The Wall Street Journal*, March 31, 2016, http://www.wsj.com/articles/secs-white-warns-silicon-valley-on-valuations-1459471580

2. Luke Reilly, "Original Minecraft Reaches 100 Million Registered Users," *IGN*, February 25, 2014, www.ign.com/articles/2014/02/26/original-minecract-reaches-100-million-registered-users

3. Joe Miller, "Microsoft Pays $2.5bn for Minecraft Maker Mojang," BBC News, September 15, 2014, www.bbc.com/news/technology-29204518

4. Eugene Kim, "The 14 Fastest Unicorns to Reach $1 Billion," *Business Insider*, August 14, 2015, http://www.businessinsider.com/fastest-startups-to-1-billion-valuation-2015-8

5. "Zynga Reports Second Quarter 2013 Financial Results," Zynga, July 25, 2013, http://investor.zynga.com/releasedetail.cfm?ReleaseID=780469

6. Belinda Luscombe, "The Troubling Rise of Facebook's Top Game Company," *Time*, November 30, 2009, http://content.time.com/time/magazine/article/0,9171,1940668,00.html

7. Startup Berkeley, "Mark Pincus talk at Startup@Berkeley." Vimeo video, March 18, 2009, https://vimeo.com/3738428

8. Scott Martin, "Startup Investors Hit the Brakes," *The Wall Street Journal*, April 14, 2016, http://www.wsj.com/articles/startup-investors-hit-the-brakes -1460676478

9. Lizette Chapman and Dina Bass, "Fidelity Writes Down Value of Corporate Software Startups," *Bloomberg*, March 1, 2016, http://www.bloomberg. com/news/articles/2016-03-01/fidelity-writes-down-value-of-corporate -software-startups

10. Dan Primack, "Term Sheet — Tuesday, March 1," *Fortune,* March 1, 2016, http://fortune.com/2016/03/01/term-sheet-tuesday-march-1/

11. Sara Ashley O'Brien, "No tech firms went public this quarter," CNN Money, March 30, 2016, http://money.cnn.com/2016/03/30/technology/no-tech -ipos-q1-2016

12. Susanna Kim, "Youngest Self-Made Female Billionaire Elizabeth Holmes in Harsh Spotlight Amid Theranos' Criminal Probe," *ABC News*, April 19, 2016, http://abcnews.go.com/Business/youngest-made-female-billionaire-elizabeth -holmes-harsh-spotlight/story?id=38508510

13. Nick Stockton, "Everything You Need to Know About the Theranos Saga So Far," *Wired*, May 4, 2016, https://www.wired.com/2016/05/everything-need -know-theranos-saga-far/

14. Christopher Weaver, John Carryrou, and Michael Siconolfi, "Walgreens Sues Theranos, Seeks $140 Million in Damages," *The Wall Street Journal*, October 16, 2016, http://www.wsj.com/articles/walgreens-seeks-to-recover-140-mil-lion-investment-from-theranos-1478642410

15. John Carryrou and Christopher Weaver, "Theranos Retreats from Blood Tests," *The Wall Street Journal*, October16, 2016, http://wwww.wsj.com/articles.ther-anos-retreats-from-blood-tests-147513848

16. Paul Daugherty, Marc Carrel-Billiard, Michael Blitz, Ari Bernstein, Renee Byrnes, Elise Cornille, Jolie Huang, Bill Lesieur, Michelle Sipics, and Steven Tiell, "Technology Vision 2016," *Accenture,* 2016, https://www.accenture. com/us-en/insight-technology-trends-2016

17. Nat Ives, "Under Armour's Kevin Plank Has Advice for Startups at SXSW: Start Making a Profit," *Advertising Age*, March 14, 2016, http://adage.com/ article/special-report-sxsw/armour-ceo-plank-advice-startups-sxsw-make-a -profit/303106/

18. Dan Primack, "Term Sheet — Monday, April 18," *Fortune*, April 18, 2016, http://fortune.com/2016/04/18/term-sheet-monday-april-18/

19. Jennifer Surane and Shannon Pettypiece, "Costco, Citi Flooded With Complaints in Rocky Card Rollout," *Bloomberg*, June 23, 2016, http://www.bloomberg.com/news/articles/2016-06-23/costco-citi-deluged-by-complaints-in-rocky-credit-card-rollout

Part II: Why Build Lovable Products?

CHAPTER 1: WHAT IS A PRODUCT?

1. Sarah Perez, "Rakuten Buys Ebates For $1 Billion," *TechCrunch*, September 9, 2014, https://techcrunch.com/2014/09/09/rakuten-buys-ebates-for-1-billion/

2. Theodore Levitt, "Marketing Success Through Differentiation—of Anything," *Harvard Business Review*, January 1980, https://hbr.org/1980/01/marketing-success-through-differentiation-of-anything

3. Geoffrey A. Moore, *Crossing the Chasm: Marketing and Selling High-Tech Products to Mainstream Customers,* (New York: HarperCollins, 2006), 227.

4. Kevin Quiring, Fabio De Angelis, Esther Gasull, Robert Wollan, Thomas Jacobson, Rob Hons, Tiffany Gilbert, and Tiago Salvador, "Digital Disconnect in Customer Engagement," *Accenture,* https://www.accenture.com/us-en/insight-digital-disconnect-customer-engagement

CHAPTER 2: PURSUING LOVE

1. Rolfe Winkler, "Airbnb nearing $1 billion in annual revenue," *The Wall Street Journal*, November 20, 2015, http://www.marketwatch.com/story/airbnb-nearing-1-billion-in-annual-revenue-2015-11-20

2. Greylock Partners, "Blitzscaling 18: Brian Chesky on Launching Airbnb and the Challenges of Scale." YouTube Video, November 30, 2015, https://youtu.be/W608u6sBFpo

3. CB Insights, "Your Startup Has a 1.28% Chance of Becoming a Unicorn," *CB Insights*, https://www.cbinsights.com/blog/unicorn-conversion-rate/

4. John Mullins, "VC Funding Can Be Bad For Your Start-Up," *Harvard Business Review*, August 4, 2014, https://hbr.org/2014/08/vc-funding-can-be-bad-for -your-start-up

5. Capital On Stage, "Bill Earner - Connect Ventures," YouTube video, March 18, 2013, https://youtu.be/C5_V-vgzy7Q

6. "2015 Benchmark Report Series: E-commerce Growth," RJMetrics, 2015, https://rjmetrics.com/resources/reports/2015-ecommerce-growth-bench-mark

7. Clayton Christensen, James Allworth, and Karen Dillon, *How Will You Measure Your Life?* (New York: HarperCollins, 2012), 240.

CHAPTER 3: THE TEN BUILDING BLOCKS OF LOVABILITY

1. Barry Schwartz, *Why We Work* (New York: Simon & Schuster/TEDBooks, 2015), 112.

2. Jeff Grubb, "Pokémon Go outpaces Clash Royale as the fastest game ever to No. 1 on the mobile revenue charts," *VentureBeat*, July 11, 2016, http://venturebeat. com/2016/07/11/pokemon-go-outpaces-clash-royale-as-the-fastest-game -ever-to-no-1-on-the-mobile-revenue-charts

3. "AT&T Caps Strong Year with 2.8 Million Wireless Net Adds and Dou-ble-Digit Growth in Revenues, Adjusted Operating Margin, Adjusted EPS and Free Cash Flow in Fourth Quarter," AT&T Newsroom, January 26, 2016, http://about.att.com/story/att_fourth_quarter_earnings_2015.html

4. "ACSI Telecommunications Report 2016," American Customer Satisfaction Index, June 1, 2016, http://www.theacsi.org/news-and-resources/customer -satisfaction-reports/reports-2016/acsi-telecommunications-report-2016

CHAPTER 4: THE BENEFITS OF BEING LOVED

1. Korn Ferry Hay Group, "World's Most Admired Companies: 2016," *Fortune*, http://fortune.com/worlds-most-admired-companies/unitedhealth-group -100000/

2. Charlotte Rogers, "How Toms engaged 3.5 million people in one day," *Marketing Week*, June 29, 2016, https://www.marketingweek.com/2016/06/29/how-foot-wear-brand-toms-engaged-3-5-million-people-in-one-day-using-tribe-power/

3. Micah Solomon, "The Rackspace Method: 'Fanatical' Customer Service And Customer Support In The B2B Cloud," *Forbes*, February 18, 2015, http://www.forbes.com/sites/micahsolomon/2015/02/18/the-rackspace-method-fanatical-customer-service-and-customer-support-in-the-b2b-cloud/#427bcf95334e

4. "Customer Rage," Center for Services Leadership at the W. P. Carey School of Business at Arizona State University, 2015, https://wpcarey.asu.edu/research/services-leadership/2004-national-customer-rage-study

5. Alex Edmans, "28 Years of Stock Market Data Shows a Link Between Employee Satisfaction and Long-Term Value," *Harvard Business Review*, March 24, 2016, https://hbr.org/2016/03/28-years-of-stock-market-data-shows-a-link-between-employee-satisfaction-and-long-term-value

6. "LinkedIn Talent Brand Index," LinkedIn Talent Solutions, https://business.linkedin.com/content/dam/business/talent-solutions/global/en_US/site/pdf/datasheets/linkedin-talent-brand-index-en-us-130829.pdf

7. Joan Voight, "Patagonia Is Taking On a Provocative 'Anti-Growth' Position: Is it all just a marketing ploy?," *AdWeek*, September 29, 2013, http://www.adweek.com/news/advertising-branding/patagonia-taking-provocative-anti-growth-position-152782

CHAPTER 5: CHASE VALUE, NOT VALUATION

1. Janet Morrissey, "No Venture Capital Needed, or Wanted," *The New York Times*, June 1, 2016, http://www.nytimes.com/2016/06/02/business/smallbusiness/no-venture-capital-needed-or-wanted.html

2. Hilary Milnes, "Saatva Is the Bootstrapped Mattress Company That Is Giving Casper a Run for Its Money," *DigiDay*, December 7, 2015, http://digiday.com/brands/saatva-bootstrapped-mattress-company-giving-caspter-run-money

3. Maya Kosoff, "A Man Who Just Sold His Startup for $575 Million in Cash Gets to Keep Every Single Penny — Here's How He Did It," *Business Insider*, July 14, 2015, http://www.businessinsider.com/how-markus-frind-bootstrapped-plentyoffish-and-sold-it-for-575-million-2015-7

4. Ryan Mac, "Clinkle Up In Smoke As Investors Want Their Money Back," *Forbes*, January 22, 2016, http://www.forbes.com/sites/ryanmac/2016/01/22/clinkle-up-in-smoke-as-investors-want-their-money-back/#5aca32bd35b6

5. Christopher Steiner, "Meet The Fastest Growing Company Ever," *Forbes*, August 12, 2010, http://www.forbes.com/forbes/2010/0830/entrepreneurs -groupon-facebook-twitter-next-web-phenom.html

6. Mashable and Jolie O'Dell, "The History of Groupon," *Forbes*, January 7, 2011, http://www.forbes.com/sites/mashable/2011/01/07/the-history-of-groupon /#7a7c96281943

7. Dan Primack, "Let's stop laughing at Groupon," *Fortune*, January 26, 2015, http://fortune.com/2015/01/26/lets-stop-laughing-at-groupon/

8. Johnathan Stempel, "Groupon sues 'once-great' IBM over patent," *Reuters*, May 9, 2016, http://www.reuters.com/article/us-ibm-groupon-idUSKCN0Y02KG

9. Leena Rao, "Stripe's new funding makes it a $5 billion company," *Fortune*, July 28, 2015, http://fortune.com/2015/07/28/stripe-visa/

10. Mark Suster, "Is Going for Rapid Growth Always Good? Aren't Startups So Much More?" *Both Sides of the Table*, September 22, 2012, https://bothsides ofthetable.com/is-going-for-rapid-growth-always-good-aren-t-startups-so -much-more-b1aee5c4e96f#

11. Patience Haggin, "Mixpanel CEO's Unicorn Dreams Take a Back Seat to Cutting Costs," *The Wall Street Journal*, April 11, 2016, http://blogs.wsj.com/ venturecapital/2016/04/11/mixpanel-ceos-unicorn-dreams-take-a-back-seat -to-cutting-costs/

12. Associated Press, "HubSpot reports 4Q loss," *Yahoo Finance*, February 10, 2016, http://finance.yahoo.com/news/hubspot-reports-4q-loss-223142681.html

13. "There's a .00006% Chance of Building a Billion Dollar Company: How This Man Did It." *First Round Review*, http://firstround.com/review/Theres-a -00006-Chance-of-Building-a-Billion-Dollar-Company-How-This-Man -Did-It/

14. Catherine Rampell, "The Odds Your Vote Will 'Make a Difference,'" *The New York Times*, October 31, 2008, http://economix.blogs.nytimes .com/2008/10/31/the-odds-that-your-vote-will-make-a-difference

15. Rohin Dhar, "How Much Do Startups Pay for Office Space?," *Priceonomics*, February 26, 2014, https://priceonomics.com/how-much-do-startups -pay-for-office-space/

16. "Latest Telecommuting Statistics," Global Workplace Analytics, January 2016, http://globalworkplaceanalytics.com/telecommuting-statistics

17. Deborah Gage, "The Venture Capital Secret: 3 Out of 4 Start-Ups Fail," *The Wall Street Journal*, September 20, 2012, http://www.wsj.com/articles/SB10 000872396390443720204578004980476429190

18. Greg Head, "Sorry, Not All Startups Should Be Funded" *Greg Head* (blog), http://greghead.com/sorry-not-all-startups-should-be-funded/

Part III: Creating Lovability

CHAPTER 6: THE OLD WAYS ARE NEW AGAIN

1. Julie Bort, "Lies, Booze, and Billions: How One of the Fastest-Growing Start-ups in Silicon Valley History Raised $580 Million Then Spiraled Out of Control," *Business Insider*, March 11, 2016, http://www.businessinsider.com/the-inside-story-of-zenefits-2016-3

2. Dan Primack, "Will Ex-Zenefits Employees Sue The Company?," *Fortune*, July 1, 2016, http://fortune.com/2016/07/01/will-ex-zenefits-employees-sue-the-company/

3. Chris Welch, "4chan founder Chris Poole is shutting down Canvas and DrawQuest for iOS," *The Verge*, January 21, 2014, http://www.theverge.com/2014/1/21/5331626/4chan-founder-chris-poole-shutting-down-canvas-drawquest

4. "$58.8 Billion in Venture Capital Invested Across U.S. in 2015, According to the MoneyTree Report," National Venture Capital Association, January 15, 2015, http://nvca.org/pressreleases/58-8-billion-in-venture-capital-invested-across-u-s-in-2015-according-to-the-moneytree-report-2/

5. Maya Kosoff, "Investors just poured $500 million into Jet.com, the buzzy Amazon-killer that's now worth $1.5 billion," *Business Insider*, November 4, 2015, http://www.businessinsider.com/jet-raises-500-million-at-a-1-billion-valuation-2015-11

6. Andrew J. Hawkins, "Tesla Has Received 325,000 Preorders for the Model 3," *The Verge*, April 7, 2016, http://www.theverge.com/2016/4/7/11385146/tesla-model-3-preorders-375000-elon-musk

7. Seth Godin, "The computer, the network and the economy," *Seth's Blog* (blog), July 7, 2016, http://sethgodin.typepad.com/seths_blog/2016/07/the -computer-the-network-and-the-economy.html

8. Laura Entis, "Where Startup Funding Really Comes From," *Entrepreneur*, November 20, 2013, https://www.entrepreneur.com/article/230011

9. Greg Bensinger, "EBay Divests Craigslist Stake, Ends Litigation," *The Wall Street Journal*, June 19, 2015, http://www.wsj.com/articles/ebay-sells-craigslist-stake -back-to-craigslist-1434730678

10. Louis Hau, "Newspaper Killer," *Forbes*, December 11, 2006, http://www.forbes .com/2006/12/08/newspaper-classifield-online-tech_cx-lh_1211craigslist .html

11. Charles Du, "4 Lessons I Learned Designing NASA's 1st iPhone App," *Aha! Blog* (blog), January 29, 2016, http://blog.aha.io/4-product-management -lessons-learned-designing-nasas-1st-iphone-app/

12. Kia Kokalitcheva, "On-Demand Startup Zirtual Will Be Back in Business Thanks to Startups.co," *Fortune*, August 12, 2015, http://fortune .com/2015/08/12/zirtual-returns-startups-co/

CHAPTER 7: THE RESPONSIVE METHOD

1. Jennifer Robison, "Why So Many New Companies Fail During Their First Five Years," *Gallup*, October 23, 2014, http://www.gallup.com/businessjournal /178787/why-new-companies-fail-during-first-five-years.aspx

2. Sam Altman and Dustin Moskorwitz "Lecture 1: How to Start a Startup," http://startupclass.samaltman.com/courses/lec01/

3. Neil Patel, "Why A Transparent Culture Is Good For Business," *Fast Company*, October 9, 2014, https://www.fastcompany.com/3036794/the-future-of -work/why-a-transparent-culture-is-good-for-business

4. Heather Boushey and Sarah Jane Glynn, "There Are Significant Business Costs to Replacing Employees," Center for American Progress, November 16, 2012, https://www.americanprogress.org/issues/labor/report/2012/11/16/44464/ there-are-significant-business-costs-to-replacing-employees/

5. Paul Leinwand, Cesare Mainardi, and Art Kleiner, "Only 8% of Leaders Are Good at Both Strategy and Execution," *Harvard Business Review,* December 30, 2015, https://hbr.org/2015/12/only-8-of-leaders-are-good-at-both-strate- gy-and-execution

6. "Our culture," Google Company, https://www.google.com/about/company/facts/culture/

CHAPTER 8: HOW TO BUILD LOVABLE PRODUCTS

1. Alex Davies, "Strava's Cycling App Is Helping Cities Build Better Bike Lanes," *Wired*, June 3, 2014, https://www.wired.com/2014/06/strava-sells-cycling-data/

2. Brian de Haaff, "4 Roadmapping Secrets From Successful Product Managers," *Aha! Blog* (blog), September 28, 2015, http://blog.aha.io/product-roadmapping-secrets/

3. "The multibillion dollar cost of poor customer service," NewVoice Media, December 12, 2013, http://www.newvoicemedia.com/en-us/news/corporate/the-multibillion-dollar-cost-of-poor-customer-service

4. Seth Godin, "Seth Godin: The Truth about Shipping," *99u*, http://99u.com/articles/6249/seth-godin-the-truth-about-shipping

5. Peter Shankman, "The Greatest Customer Service Story Ever Told, Starring Morton's Steakhouse," *Peter Shankman*, August 18, 2011, http://shankman.com/the-greatest-customer-service-story-ever-told-starring-mortons-steakhouse/

6. Christina McMenemy, "A Crazy Example of Great Service," *A Mommy Story*, March 1, 2012, http://www.amommystory.com/2012/03/a-crazy-example-of-great-service.html."

7. "So LEGO Did a Pretty Neat Thing," *Buzzfeed*, November 29, 2012, https://www.buzzfeed.com/svoip/why-lego-is-the-best-company-in-the-world-4y59

8. Kyle Cassidy, "The Story Behind Our Most Popular Email," *Simple* (blog), January 25, 2016, https://www.simple.com/company/email-story

CHAPTER 9: BEING A LOVABLE COMPANY

1. Jeff Chu, "Toms Sets Out To Sell A Lifestyle, Not Just Shoes," *Fast Company*, June 17, 2013, https://www.fastcompany.com/3012568/blake-mycoskie-toms

2. Sheryl Garratt, "Toms' Blake Mycoskie Brews Up in NYC," *Observer*, February 27, 2015, http://observer.com/2015/02/toms-blake-mycoskie-brews-up-in-nyc/

3. Stephanie Strom, "At Chobani, Now It's Not Just the Yogurt That's Rich," *The New York TImes*, April 26, 2016, http://www.nytimes.com/2016/04/27/business/a-windfall-for-chobani-employees-stakes-in-the-company.html

4. Stephen F. Freeman, "Effects of ESOP Adoption and Employee Ownership: Thirty years of Research and Experience," University of Pennsylvania Center for Organizational Dynamics, January 4, 2007, http://repository.upenn.edu/cgi/viewcontent.cgi?article=1001&context=od_working_papers

5. John Cook, "Full memo: Jeff Bezos responds to brutal NYT story, says it doesn't represent the Amazon he leads," *GeekWire*, August 16, 2015, http://www.geekwire.com/2015/full-memo-jeff-bezos-responds-to-cutting-nyt-expose-says-tolerance-for-lack-of-empathy-needs-to-be-zero/

6. Brie Weiler Reynolds, "Survey: Only 7% of Workers Say They're Most Productive in the Office," FlexJobs, August 26, 2016, https://www.flexjobs.com/blog/post/survey-workers-most-productive-in-the-office/

7. Kara Swisher and Evan Ramstad, "Yahoo! to Announce Acquisition Of Broadcast.com for $5.7 Billion," *The Wall Street Journal*, April 1, 1999, http://www.wsj.com/articles/SB929916873273123235

8. Lars Dalgaard, "Thoughts on Building Weatherproof Companies," *a16z Blog* (blog), March 25, 2016, http://a16z.com/2016/03/25/building-weatherproof-companies/

9. Leena Rao, "After Closing $3.4B Acquisition Of SuccessFactors, SAP Pushes Human Capital Management In The Cloud," *TechCrunch*, February 22, 2012, https://techcrunch.com/2012/02/22/successfactors-sap/

10. Frank Witsil, *Detroit Free Press*, "Call Center Jobs Increase as More Return from Overseas," *USA Today*, August 4, 2014, http://www.usatoday.com/story/money/business/2014/08/04/call-center-jobs-overseas/13560107/

CHAPTER 10: THE LOVABILITY TOOLKIT

1. Jason Hall, "There's Good and Bad in Chipotle's Mexican Grill's Latest Earnings," *The Motley Fool*, October 27, 2016, http://www.fool.com/investing/2016/10/27/theres-good-and-bad-in-chipotle-mexican-grills-lat.aspx

INDEX

ABOUT THE AUTHOR

Brian de Haaff is the co-founder and CEO of Aha! — one of the fastest growing companies in the U.S. and the world's #1 product roadmap software. His two previous startups were acquired by well-known public companies. He writes and speaks about product and company growth and the adventure of living a meaningful life. Brian is a proud graduate of both The University of California at Berkeley and Northwestern University. He lives in Silicon Valley with his wife and three sons. *Lovability* is his first book.

To learn more or contact Brian, visit aha.io/lovability